cebu
furniture

A HISTORY OF INSPIRATION AND INNOVATION

cebu furniture

A HISTORY OF INSPIRATION AND INNOVATION

Text by
Maricris Encarnacion

ARTPOSTASIA

cebu furniture

A HISTORY OF INSPIRATION AND INNOVATION

WRITER: Maricris Encarnacion

MANAGING EDITORS: Jacqueline Joan Arquiza and Melody Gocheco Wigforss

CREATIVE DIRECTOR: Tina Colayco

DESIGNER: Katrina Palomo Garcia

ASSISTANT DESIGNER / COORDINATOR: Rina Camacho

CEBU PROJECT CONSULTANT: Ruby Babao-Salutan

PROJECT ASSISTANTS: Cecilia Francia Botor, Cyndi Camagay

PRODUCED BY: ArtPostAsia Pte Ltd
Email: info@artpostasia.com
www.artpostasia.com

Hard Cover ISBN 978-971-0579-14-3
Soft Cover ISBN 978-971-0579-08-2

Page 1: Bird's Nest Coffee Table made of rattan poles with aluminum legs, designed by Fernando "Astik" Villarin, manufactured by Pacific Traders & Manufacturing Corp., 2008.

Page 2: Voyage Daybed made of solid polyethylene and steel, part of the Voyage Collection on p. 156, designed by Kenneth Cobonpue, manufactured by Interior Crafts of the Islands Inc.

Above: Detail of Stingray Lounging Chair, designed by Michel Guinefolleau, manufactured by Cebu Intertrade Export (full details on p. 256).

contents

foreword   6
introduction   9

an industry is born   18

rattan revolution   34

from trading to manufacturing   46

growth and expansion   66

designing for the world   92
cebu furniture global gallery

afterword   268
photo timeline   276
index   280
photo credits   286
cfif directory   288
acknowledgments   296

foreword
charles streegan

The Cebu furniture industry had its early stirrings in the 1920s. Since then, it has achieved tremendous growth, taken a remarkable course of successes and weathered challenges that have transformed and touched many lives, businesses and the province of Cebu itself.

While the history of the industry continues to be written, many of us today, including myself, feel privileged to have first-hand experience of the industry's most important milestones and memorable years. This book is a tribute to the industry, an appreciation of its history and a recognition of the many remarkable and passionate people who pioneered, blazed new trails and catapulted Cebu furniture design and manufacturing into today's global arena.

The following chronological narrative of the industry is complemented by a visual story, featuring the iconic furniture and home accessory pieces to have made waves in local and foreign markets, in the past six decades of the Cebu furniture industry. At every junction in time, each of the featured products shows evolution and innovation, from the standpoint of indigenous materials, design and the

Bottom: Photos from the 1994 Cebu X

craftsmanship of Filipinos. Over time, the industry established its identity for quality production, which has attracted sophisticated customers and markets from every corner of the world.

Since its inception, the industry has shown local and international audiences the amazing levels of creativity and the passion of Filipino craftsmen and entrepreneurs, which has endured and prevailed during the best and worst of times. The Cebu furniture industry has always shown resilience in the face of adversity and flexibility by forging ahead to focus on the needs and standards demanded by various markets.

For this book, we worked as closely as possible with the various key manufacturers of furniture in Cebu, as well as the Cebu Furniture Industries Foundation (CFIF) and the industry's international partners and buyers.

Bottom: 2011 Cebu NEXT (left); CFIF Board of Trustees for 2010-2011

The challenges the industry faces – excess capacity, renewed competition from our neighbors and a more discerning public – cannot be ignored. It is our hope and goal that this book serves as an inspiring reference for the past, present and future.

introduction
maricris encarnacion

W hile the Philippines boasts of various cities known for manufacturing furniture using a variety of indigenous materials, Cebu City, in particular, has successfully grown and developed its furniture industry in the last 60 years, carving out distinctive niche markets around the world.

Cebu manufactured, for example, the McGuire "bamboo" table that sat in the foyers of the White House in Washington, DC during the term of President Richard Nixon. In 1983, U.S. President Ronald Reagan and UK Prime Minister Margaret Thatcher were photographed sitting on McGuire rattan arm chairs made in Cebu. John and Elinor McGuire, who were former residents of the Philippines, were among the very first international buyers of Cebu rattan furniture since the 1950s.

Fast forward to 2004, Cebu-based internationally acclaimed designer Kenneth Cobonpue's C-U-C-ME screen made a cameo appearance in the Hollywood movie Wimbledon. In 2007, Cobonpue was commissioned to put together an entire film set with his furniture for the hit movie Ocean's 13.

Opposite page: The lobby of Crimson Resort and Spa in Mactan, Cebu.

Elsewhere around the world, markets welcomed the high quality, design and excellent craftsmanship of furniture made in Cebu. The province became a destination for furniture production, on top of being a favorite vacation and tourist spot.

CEBU AND ITS STRATEGIC LOCATION

The Philippines is an archipelago of 7,107 islands divided into three main island groups – Luzon in the north, Mindanao in the south and Visayas at the center. Unlike the other two groups dominated by a single large mass of land, the Visayas includes seven major islands further divided into the political regions of Eastern, Western and Central Visayas.

Cebu is strategically located at the heart of Central Visayas, making it a natural geographical hub for inter-island trade and commerce. Narrow coastlines, limestone plateaus and rugged mountain ranges traversing the middle of the island from north to south, characterize the Cebu mainland – rendering it unfriendly to agriculture due to its lack of arable flat land.

Its people, therefore, founded their homes on the coast and the hills, living off the sea as fishermen and seafarers and establishing businesses focused on trade and manufacturing. This largely non-agricultural local economy has spawned a large pool of skilled workers trained through education, experience and tradition.

Today, shipping, tourism and manufacturing are the main drivers of Cebu's economy. The majority of shipping companies in the Philippines, including those engaged in shipbuilding, are based in Cebu. Not surprisingly, a large concentration of highly skilled Filipino seamen who find overseas employment in international vessels come from the province.

Cebu, with its beautiful beaches, excellent dive spots and warm people, continues to distinguish itself as one of the top domestic and foreign tourist destinations in the Philippines. It has likewise given rise to a vibrant hospitality industry and a world-class labor force trained in the hotel, food service, recreation and entertainment industries.

Above: Cebu is known for its beautiful beaches, making it one of the top tourist destinations in the Philippines. Crimson Resort and Spa, Mactan, Cebu.

Right: Mangoes and shells are famous exports of Cebu.

From the late 1940s, rattan poles found their way to Cebu and played an important part in the furniture industry's growth.

Left: Unprocessed rattan poles with skin in the early stages of the manufacturing production line.

Below: Processed rattan poles.

In 1521, Ferdinand Magellan landed in what was then known as Sugbu (now Cebu). He planted a huge cross to commemorate the first baptism on the island, that of Rajah Humabon. Today, part of this original cross is displayed in a cross made of *tindalo* wood, in a chapel beside the Basilica Minore del Santo Niño, Cebu.

In the manufacturing sector, Cebu's workers are regarded among the most productive in the country, providing one of the many reasons why multinational companies build their factories in special economic zones developed by the national government. Cebu has one of the biggest, if not the biggest, furniture clusters in the country, responsible for producing a big portion of the Philippines' furniture exports. It ranks among the top furniture exporters to the U.S. and has made inroads in the European, Middle Eastern and Japanese markets. It has gained a global reputation as a top producer of fine furniture and has made a pitch to be the Design Destination of Asia.

Much of Cebu's rich history can be traced as far back as 400 years ago when the Portuguese explorer Ferdinand Magellan led a Spanish expedition that blazed a new route to the East across the Pacific Ocean. Magellan never reached the Moluccas, but he was the first European to reach what is now known as the Philippines, landing in the island of Cebu on March 16, 1521.

The "Sinulog Festival" is one of Cebu's most popular annual celebrations in honor of the Infant Jesus (Santo Niño). The Sinulog festivities consist of a religious procession and a grand street parade of costumed residents and devotees holding a Santo Niño.

It was however another expedition led by the Spaniard Miguel Lopez de Legazpi almost 50 years later, that the first Spanish settlement in the country – La Villa del Santisimo Nombre de Jesus – was established. When Legazpi landed in Cebu in 1565, he found a people belonging to a cultured society, that had its own justice system, music, wooden houses with rooms, and its own units of weights and measures using wooden balances.

Legazpi found natives engaged in brisk trading with Chinese and Malay merchants, using livestock, rice and gold to barter. Legazpi immediately distributed the first *encomiendas*, or land trusts, to the colonists to establish the first communities under the Spanish Crown. The new *encomiendas* were designed to establish government, schools and residences, at the center of which was the town church that ensured the spread of the Catholic faith.

Cebu is one of the top furniture exporters to the U.S. and has gained a global reputation as a producer of fine furniture.

It was through the Church that the Spanish colonizers captured the hearts and minds of the Filipinos, making God and the Church, the center of people's lives.

Local artists and artisans learned and thrived, painting and carving beautiful religious images of the Holy Family, Jesus, angels and saints for both the church and devotees. These were copied from icons and pictures brought by the religious orders from Spain.

Centuries of exposure to religious Western art exercised its aesthetic influence on the Filipinos. Cebu grew with Spanish-style town plazas and many churches would be constructed along coastal communities from north to south.

Cebu's history and demography have therefore defined the unique mix of peoples and culture of Cebu.

Opposite page and below: Sushi Lounge Chair (with detail and variations). Made of rattan frame with bamboo flooring and yellow leather binding, it was designed by University of the Philippines student Mae Arrolado, 2009.

The story of the beginnings, rise and continuing evolution of the Cebu furniture industry draws strongly from such a historical backdrop. The latter provides the references for traditions of skilled craftsmanship, new cycles of migrations, and strong trade and commercial acumen of industry players.

As the story of the Cebu furniture industry unfolds, the personal and professional journeys of people are brought back to life for their exemplary contributions to an industry that has become a source of pride for Cebuanos and Filipinos.

The development of the Cebu furniture industry in this publication follows a chronological storyline, with the provenances of iconic pieces by respected members of the industry.

an industry
is born

I t was the end of World War II and people were eager to return to their normal everyday lives. Cebu, as in most places in the Philippines, was teeming with American servicemen tasked to keep the peace and provide security. One of them was U.S. Army Major Clarence Gushurst, a native of Florida, a state that was largely tropical and where rattan furniture was commonly used for outdoor porches and patios. He took an interest in rattan and while in Cebu, found a few shops that made rattan furniture. He managed to convince Doña Maria Montenegro Aboitiz of Cebu to partner with him in the rattan furniture business. In 1947, they established Mehitabel Furniture Company, with a workshop in Doña Maria's backyard. She knew very little about the business but easily learned the ropes with her workers. When Major Gushurst returned to the U.S., Doña Maria continued the business on her own.

The years following the end of World War II also brought a number of American companies and their expatriates to Cebu. Many of them chose to settle in Cebu and became part of the local community. They looked for opportunities to create new businesses for themselves and their new Filipino friends.

Pages 18-19: Binding furniture with rawhide leather, a technique patented worldwide by the McGuire Furniture Company with a guarantee that bindings will not loosen, break, or tear. In the Philippines, Mehitabel Furniture Inc. was the first to use this technique when it started to collaborate with McGuire.

bilibid

MATERIAL: rattan frame with wicker weaving
MANUFACTURER: mehitabel furniture inc.
YEAR: 1920s

The chair is named after Bilibid Prison in Muntinlupa, Metro Manila, whose inmates made them. The design of the Bilibid chair is very hardy and cool – a perfect combination for the tropics.

John McGuire was then a young executive for Standard Vacuum Oil in Cebu. He forged a friendship with Mrs. Aboitiz, and his fascination for rattan grew with the number of hours he spent observing the Cebuano workers manually manipulate the poles with captivating skill and grace.

Like most enterprising Filipino mothers with young children to raise in post-war times, Doña Maria worked from the house. Her showroom was her home, with furniture sold off the floor. Daughter Josephine reminisces with amusement the many afternoons she would return from school to an empty house, with all their furniture shipped off to a buyer. They had to live with the inconvenience until Doña Maria's furniture makers completed replacements. Relief was short-lived since furniture was sold just as quickly as they were made. It was a sign that business was good, and the children were not expected to complain.

Meanwhile, John McGuire realized he didn't want to pursue his corporate career. He moved back to the U.S., married his fiancée Elinor, and searched for a business that would allow him and his wife to work together. They had a one-time opportunity to trade a warehouse full of bulky rattan furniture that most people bought to use in their sun porches.

McGuire remembered his days at Doña Maria's little factory observing the workers, marveling at the many forms that the poles could be twisted and bent into. He knew that rattan was strong and flexible, cheap and durable, never warped despite manipulation. He was convinced that when designed properly, rattan furniture had a strong potential to join the realm of fine quality furniture. Without formal training in furniture design, John and Elinor eschewed bulk and conceptualized a light rattan piece, sending the illustration to Doña Maria in Cebu. She responded that their design was not strong enough, insisting that it was bulk that gave rattan furniture their strength. This proved to be a challenge to McGuire.

He found inspiration in the movies, specifically the Western cowboy genre. He remembered seeing the cowboys use wet rawhide to slowly strangle their enemies. Once the leather binding started to dry, it would tighten the noose around the neck. This simple principle gave John McGuire the inspiration to develop and apply a furniture construction method strengthening dowel-wedged joints by wrapping them with wet rawhide bindings. As the rawhide dried, the joints became tautly bound together, giving the furniture unsurpassed durability, and an added touch of clean aesthetics. This technique of binding rattan with rawhide has been patented worldwide and guarantees that the bindings will not loosen, break, or tear, a discovery that revolutionized the construction of rattan furniture.

John and Elinor McGuire set up the McGuire Furniture Company in San Francisco, California in 1948. McGuire began a successful collaboration that would span decades with Doña Maria Aboitiz, whose little workshop would grow with McGuire's vision and designs.

John and Elinor McGuire with Josephine Aboitiz Booth in 1987.

THE PIONEERS

MEHITABEL AND MCGUIRE

The history of Mehitabel Furniture Inc. is intertwined with that of McGuire Furniture Company, one story incomplete without the other. John and Elinor McGuire and Doña Maria Aboitiz collaborated in developing furniture targeted at a more upscale U.S. market, using McGuire's patented rawhide binding technique. John and Elinor worked together to develop furniture of perfect proportion and design, using the finest natural materials and meticulous workmanship.

McGuire's first big break came when he was able to convince renowned interior designer Eleanor Forbes of the famous Gump's in San Francisco to design furniture using rattan. When he first approached Forbes, she rejected all his pieces simply because she found them unattractive. Unfazed by this setback and armed with an unwavering belief in rattan's potential, McGuire eventually managed to convince her to work with rattan her own way. Forbes' 15 designs were a success. Two of these

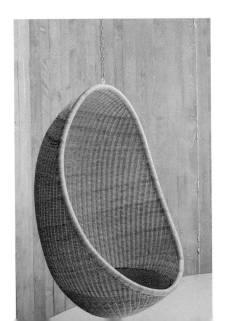

egg

MATERIAL: wicker
SIZE: H 125.1 x W 85.1 cm
DESIGNER: nanna ditzel
MANUFACTURER: mehitabel furniture inc.
CLIENT: exclusively to bonacina pierantonio (italy)
YEAR: 1959

This chair was inspired by the round and unpretentious shape of an egg.

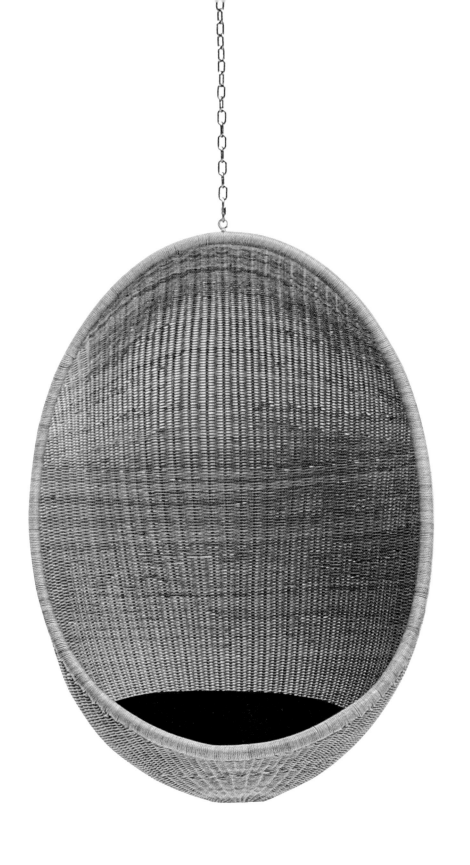

designs are considered classics and are today displayed at the Museum of Modern Art in New York. Rattan furniture from Cebu, particularly from Mehitabel, became the center of McGuire's business.

Josephine Aboitiz Booth, Doña Maria's daughter, recalls when John McGuire took an interest in Cebu's rattan furniture, he took it to the U.S. and said to a famous designer, "You know, I saw the most beautiful material – with the worst designs, in my life". At that time rattan was lashed together with rattan split – strips of bark or skin, which became loose with use and time. McGuire commissioned talented designers and worked with Mehitabel to produce elegant rattan furniture fit for the homes of the truly wealthy with discerning taste. John and Elinor moved rattan furniture from the realm of the common and inexpensive, to that of high class and luxury – with Mehitabel as the McGuire Furniture Company's major manufacturing partner. Florentino Atillo, then working as production manager, was instrumental in

arm chair

MATERIALS: rattan and rawhide bindings
SIZE: H 96.5 x W 53.3 x D 55.9 cm
FINISH: natural or dark varnish
DESIGNER: elinor mcguire
STYLISTIC VARIATIONS: side chair
MANUFACTURER: mehitabel furniture inc.
CLIENT: exclusive to the mcguire furniture company
YEAR: 1968

The rattan rugbeater, which is used to beat the dust off rugs while they hung from a clothesline, was the inspiration for this arm chair.

executing John McGuire's designs perfectly. McGuire remembers him fondly as, "the man who made things possible".

Josephine joined Mehitabel in 1970 and immediately took control of the business. When she was 16, she was sent by her mother, Doña Maria Aboitiz, to the U.S. to study Interior Design in Los Angeles, California. Upon her return, her mother didn't bother with transition, practically dumping outstanding commissions and workload on her lap, confident in Josephine's ability to execute a plan of action best for the company.

Josephine expanded Mehitabel beyond its traditional markets in the U.S. by exporting furniture to customers in Japan, Europe and Australia. With her at the helm, the relationship between Mehitabel and the McGuire Furniture Company continued to prosper. Family ties and connections were real and valuable to both the Aboitiz and McGuire families, and the bond between them began to transcend business and became very personal. Each family member became part of the other's extended family, and business and family trips were soon one and the same.

gothic collection
console table

MATERIAL: rattan
SIZE: H 71.1 x W 182.9 x D 45.7 cm
FINISH: light or dark varnish
DESIGNER: elinor mcguire
STYLISTIC VARIATIONS: headboard, chair
MANUFACTURER: mehitabel furniture inc.
CLIENT: exclusive to the mcguire furniture company
YEAR: 1970s

The Gothic Movement influenced the architecture of most of the great cathedrals, castles and universities in Europe. Gothic pointed arches and ribbed vaulting inspired this simple but well-designed console.

Josephine's son, Robert, grew up spending many summers at the factory. It was his playground and the machines and workers his toys and playmates. As he grew older, he worked a few summers doing odd jobs. In the mid-1980s he returned to Cebu, after years of studying and working in the U.S., seamlessly getting into the rhythm of Mehitabel. He was destined for business and became the third generation of the Aboitiz family to run the company.

The short supply of rattan became a major concern to the company in the late 1980s, as manufacturing revolved exclusively around this material. Mehitabel invested in a pilot project to produce wooden cabinets and case goods designed to complement rattan furniture, so a new line could be sold to existing customers. It proved to be a success – hence Linea Fina was formed in the mid-1990s with its own production facility. While each business had its own distinct customer base at the start, increasing capabilities of both facilities created a synergy and a convergence of customer base. In 2005, Linea Fina merged with Mehitabel – which continues to produce quality high-end furniture for residential and contract markets throughout the world.

ATILLO'S RATTAN & WOOD INDUSTRIES, INC. (ARWII)

Florentino Rallos Atillo was an officer in the army during World War II. When the war ended in 1945, he became an instructor at the Cebu School of Arts and Trade – teaching vocational students how to make furniture. When Maria Aboitiz established Mehitabel in 1947, she approached Atillo to train her workers and eventually hired him to become the company's first production manager.

In the meantime, Florentino Rallos Atillo and his wife Narcisa Lopez started a cottage industry style of business in 1948. It was the fulfillment of his vision for social responsibility – teaching Cebuanos how to make a living, by building skills and providing them with a market for their work. He trained those who chose to work for him how to make furniture and accessories made of rattan, *buri*, and *capiz*. His backyard was not big enough to house his workers, so he trained them to work from home and asked them to bring the finished products to his house. During this time, he was also the full-time production manager of Mehitabel, so his wife fulfilled her role as business partner full-time and also learned how to make furniture.

When Atillo left Mehitabel in the mid-1950s, he and his wife established Atillo's House of Rattan, on P. del Rosario St., which sold rattan and *buri* furniture – as well as *capiz* lamps and accessories to the local market. They then built a factory in Banilad, considered the hinterlands as it was located far from the center of the city. Atillo's House of Rattan started exporting in the late 1950s and got a big break when the Government Service Administrator (GSA) for U.S. military bases, Tai Chong of Honolulu, Hawaii, placed an initial order for furniture. Atillo's furniture passed rigid standards of quality control, which in the 1960s consisted of dropping the pieces from a certain height – usually several floors up – and the furniture would be approved if it didn't fall apart. Atillo's House of Rattan was soon supplying all the furniture for American military bases worldwide. The company went on to establish lucrative business relationships with Ficks Reed Rattan and O'Asian in the U.S. and

Garry Masters in Australia. In 1968, the company received its first Presidential Award – Top Furniture Manufacturer in the Philippines – from President Ferdinand Marcos.

Florentino and Narcisa's son Florentino III started working in his parents' factory at the age of 17. In 1969, the company was renamed Atillo's Rattan and Wood Industries, Inc. (ARWII). That same year Florentino died, leaving the business to his wife Narcisa, with his now 19-year old son Florentino III managing the factory. By 1976, Florentino Atillo III left ARWII to set up his own business – Atillo Manufacturing Corporation (AMANCOR) – with his wife Irma. His brother, also named Florentino but nicknamed Reylan, continued to run ARWII with their mother until 1986, when they sold the property where the factory stood and proceeded to close the furniture business altogether. Although complicated family dynamics eventually led to the company's demise, ARWII continues to be remembered as one of the industry's pioneers.

RATTAN ORIGINALS INC. (NOW CASA CEBUANA)

Guillermo Figueroa was a local handicraft trader who saw the strategic positioning of Cebu as a center for inter-island shipping and trade. Born in Pasig, Rizal near Manila, he moved to Cebu to make his fortune and his clientele during this period were American GIs returning home after the war.

Being an astute businessman, he saw the potential of introducing locally made products to the American market. As his business grew during the 1950s, he decided to invest in a small workshop along the beach in Talisay, which eventually became the site for his factory. Since he had limited funds, Guillermo began production with two or three workers, a planner, a hacksaw and some rattan poles.

Initially, he focused on trading locally crafted furniture and accessories made from *buri* and rattan. As demand increased, he seized the opportunity to transform his

Guillermo Figueroa inspecting rattan poles at the factory grounds of Rattan Originals Inc.

business from trading to manufacturing and invested a large portion of his savings. As a result of his perseverance in this difficult venture, he was able to establish Rattan Originals Inc. – which soon became one of the leading manufacturers of rattan furniture.

It was only a matter of time before the world began to take notice of Cebu and its craftsmanship. And Rattan Originals Inc. used this opportunity to establish and create a market between the U.S., Mexico, West Germany, Japan, Australia, Greece, France, Italy and the Caribbean. One successful project was a hotel in Cancun, Mexico, the site for the 1981 summit meeting. Another one of the company's successes was a hotel in Greece, which needed furnishings for 200 rooms. In 1982, Rattan Originals Inc. was awarded the first-ever Golden Shell Award for excellence in exports.

With the impending shortage of rattan poles, Guillermo saw the need to diversify. In 1986, he changed the name of his company from Rattan Originals to Casa Cebuana. This strategy bolstered the company's success – not only in rattan, but also in wood manufacturing.

To this day, Casa Cebuana remains one of the leading manufacturers of high-end quality furniture in the Philippines and continues to export to the U.S., Europe, the Middle East, South America and South Africa. The company is now under the leadership of Angela Figueroa-Paulin, Guillermo's daughter. An individual with a firm belief in excellence, as well as a commitment to quality, Angela has made major investments in the company to ensure its continued success.

Aside from his business acumen, Guillermo was known for having contributed to the improvement of the skills of the Cebu furniture industry's workforce. For this and many other contributions, he is considered one of the industry's pillars.

rattan
revolution

RATTAN IN CEBU

From the late 1940s to the mid-50s, rattan poles mostly from Mindanao found their way to furniture towns within the region and in Cebu, Iloilo, and Pampanga, or were sold and shipped overseas as export raw material. Around this time in Cebu, there were many furniture shops – which could only be classified as cottage industry types – that later began to create and produce beautifully designed and handcrafted rattan furniture which met the standards and demands of Western consumers. Rattan took its place in fancy furniture catalogues and could now be seen in high-end circles throughout the world.

More than 300 plant species in the Philippines are classified as rattan, but only 30 have been identified for varied commercial purposes. This fast-growing vine-like plant is found mostly in Asian countries such as the Philippines, Indonesia and Malaysia. Although it belongs to the family of palms (palmae), rattan leaves are not bunched into a crown. Rather, rattan grows long, whip-like barbed ends which enable the plant to grow upwards and find its way to the top of the rainforest canopy for light. Its stem, or trunk, can grow as high as more than one hundred meters. Sharp with thorns, it is this stem which is the source of the rattan canes prepared for trade.

It is this rattan pole – the end product made from the slender trunks of the rattan plant – which has found so much use in furniture manufacturing, specifically for the framework of chairs and tables. When taken apart in strips, rattan can be woven into baskets, mats, carpets and many other decorative items. The appeal of rattan has always been its toughness and pliability. All of its growth fibers run lengthwise, making it much tougher than wood. But as a tropical material, it is light, durable and versatile and has a most natural appeal. Initially, it was also marketed as cheaper than any Philippine hard wood – such as narra, yakal, molave, or bagras (southern mahogany).

The type of rattan traded in Cebu grew in the dense tropical forest floors of Mindanao. Cebu, being the vibrant trade center closest to Mindanao, became a major supplier

Pages 34-35:
Rattan bent for use in furniture shows its toughness and pliability, the main appeal of the material.

Opposite page:
Rattan is a vine that grows along the ground and into the trees. Considered an invasive weed in many countries, it is solid and can be bent with the application of heat.

OF PALMS & WEAVES

The *buri* palm (*Corypha elata Roxb.*), whose leaves spread out in the large, circular shape of an open fan, is abundant in central and western Visayas – where it is used as a source of food and fiber. Three different kinds of fibers – *buri*, raffia and buntal – are obtained from the *buri* palm and are woven into home and fashion accessories, as well as furniture.

In the 1970s, *buri* furniture weavers in Cebu were clustered in the Lahug area of the city. Bernie Maduzia, a buyer from Pier 1 Imports, visited Cebu frequently, ordering handicrafts and seashells from Castilex Industrial Corporation. On one such visit, Bernie passed through the streets of Lahaug and *buri* furniture caught his eye. Stopping for a closer look, he discovered a potential market hit. Soon after, Castilex started exporting the Maharlika chair to Pier 1 in bulk. A design upgrade was developed and the Maharajah chair then became the major export item. Othello Gamallo, son of one of the founders of Castilex, recalls that the set of four saucer chairs and table were also bestsellers. Another design evolution, the Princess chair, was the last major *buri* furniture product to also be a success. By the late 1970s, exports of *buri* had declined – partly because of cutthroat competition – but largely because of the oil crisis, which pushed shipping costs to record highs. The cost of freight had become higher than the cost of the *buri* furniture and it no longer made sense to continue to export.

Buri fiber was also used by Elinor McGuire, the wife and business partner of John McGuire, for one of the McGuire Furniture Company's designs targeted at the more upscale U.S. market. Mehitabel set up a separate production line to weave *buri* using high-quality standards to meet McGuire's commitment to excellence in materials and craftsmanship. Although Elinor's design satisfied her customers' tastes, *buri* as a material did not fare well in America's outdoor weather – failing to survive the winter season. As a result, the McGuire's U.S. clientele soon rejected it. Even a later attempt to reintroduce *buri* to the U.S. market using a well-designed knockdown piece, became very difficult and was eventually abandoned.

Locally, the iconic Princess throne chair made of *buri* became a long-time favorite of many Filipinos across cities and towns in the country.

maharajah chair

MATERIALS: *buri* midribs, split and rattan poles,
black plastic strips
FINISH: natural or lacquered
DESIGNERS: quirico f. gamallo
STYLISTIC VARIATIONS: in single or double weave and
twisted or barrel base
MANUFACTURER: gamallosons traders inc.
YEAR: 1970

The Maharajah chair was inspired by thrones of royalty.

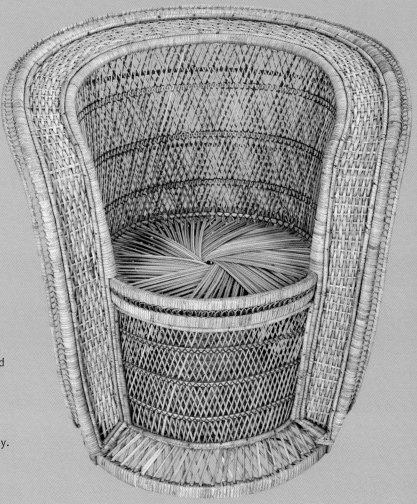

cracked ice chair

MATERIAL: rattan
SIZE: H 91.4 x W 55.9 x D 61 cm
DESIGNER: elinor mcguire
MANUFACTURER: mehitabel furniture inc.
CLIENT: exclusive to the mcguire furniture company
YEAR: 1968

This design is famous for its distinct back, an oval that frames a series of smaller lengths to create the illusion of cracked ice. The classical style of the design is timeless, giving the impression of understated elegance.

of local rattan and local entrepreneurs began to engage in the business of buying, selling and using rattan.

In the early 1970s, five rattan suppliers – namely Mindanao Rattan Corporation, Standard Rattan, Alenter Cane, Pacific Traders and Norkis Trading – exported raw poles. Local furniture manufacturers competed with the export traders for rattan, a situation deemed detrimental to the local industry. Manufacturers were experiencing a short supply of rattan to fill their orders. And Cebu – which by then was producing a vast amount of rattan furniture in the wake of Mehitabel's success and further new entries in the industry – was dependent on plantations and harvests from forests in Mindanao. In 1976, active lobbying by Cebu industry members, led by Josephine Aboitiz Booth, the Chamber of Furniture Industries of the Philippines and Asian export furniture groups, resulted in an export ban of rattan poles. Not to be proverbially beaten, the five suppliers of rattan poles joined the industry – this time as manufacturers of their own furniture. They soon were among the industry's leaders in Cebu.

Rattan's star kept shining, as foreign markets welcomed their favorite material by adopting innovative styles and trends. The timing seemed to be right, with a new 1980s generation of creative entrepreneurs, designers, manufacturers and most

butterfly chair

MATERIALS: rattan and rawhide bindings
SIZE: H 88.9 x W 82.6 x D 53.3 cm
FINISH: gold leaf
DESIGNER: edward tuttle
MANUFACTURER: mehitabel furniture inc.
CLIENT: exclusive to the mcguire furniture company
YEAR: 1979

Inspired by a Greek twig chair which the McGuires found on one of their travels to the Greek Isles where they had purchased a villa, the Butterfly chair makes for a beautiful and elegant conversation piece.

palasan
dining set

MATERIAL: palasan (species of rattan used in natural form with nodes and skin on)
SIZE: dining table base H 71.8 x Dia 60.7 cm (top) and Dia. 66 cm (bottom); dining side chair H 91.4 x W 43.2 x D 53.3 cm
DESIGNERS: john and elinor mcguire
STYLISTIC VARIATIONS: tables come in various shapes and sizes (round, rectangular or polygonal)
MANUFACTURER: tables by mindanao rattan corporation, chairs by mehitabel furniture inc.
CLIENT: exclusive to the mcguire furniture company
YEAR: 1979

The table was inspired by the form of a giant sheaf of wheat. Handcrafted in rattan, the poles are cinched in the middle by a heavy braid of rattan. The chairs complement the design of the table.

significantly, buyers, coming in from all over the world. The transformation of rattan became possible with exploration in design, experimentation, research, applications of new technologies in various processes of manufacturing and a ready market. Rattan found itself in the company of other local materials such as *abaca*, grass, bamboo and wood. The new designs called for a marrying of compatible and even incompatible materials.

Rattan runs an adventurous and parallel tale of success and survival with the history of the Cebu furniture industry. It is an essentially significant natural material which speaks of its Philippine origins, and with a versatility that has fired the imaginations of designers and inspired craftsmen to use it in both traditional and non-traditional ways. It has continuously metamorphosed through the best and the worst of times, along with economic and life cycles of plenty and drought.

Rattan's twin tale tells of the cycle of change and the interdependence of dominant designs, process innovations, market demands and the state of the world economy. It moves with the story of the industry presently facing tough competition from Indonesia and China and a worldwide economic downturn, adversely affecting the industry as a whole. But rattan is a strong and tenacious material. It will hold its place and continue to re-establish its versatile functions through the ingenuity of artists and craftsmen.

rattan target (tm)
arm chair

MATERIAL: rattan
SIZE: H 91.4 x W 60.7 x D 55.9 cm
FINISH: various, at times the circle is bronzed
DESIGNERS: john and elinor mcguire
STYLISTIC VARIATIONS: side chair
MANUFACTURER: mehitabel furniture inc.
CLIENT: exclusive to the mcguire furniture company
YEAR: 1981

The simplicity of this sophisticated and classical design with good finishes catapulted rattan to the high end of the American market.

from
trading
to
manufacturing

PACIFIC TRADERS & MANUFACTURING CORPORATION

Hugo C. Streegan, Jr. was an insurance executive when he was assigned to Cebu in 1962 as his company's Vice President for Southern Philippines. While sitting in the Executive and Loans Committee of Insular Bank of Cebu, he was exposed to potential investments that could prove profitable to a start-up group. Keen to establish his own business, his strong entrepreneurial spirit was eager to be given the chance to soar. With seven other friends, each person contributing an investment of P8,000, the Pacific Traders & Manufacturing Corporation (PTMC) was founded in 1973.

Pages 46-47: Cebu's exquisite handmade furniture require highly skilled workers who constantly redefines the phrase "attention to detail".

Opposite page: Detail of basket made from rattan peel and split. Designed by Pilar Streegan for Pacific Traders & Manufacturing Corp., 2010.

They first started by applying for a license to harvest and cut rattan poles in eastern Mindanao, subsequently exporting the rattan poles. In 1976, when the government placed a ban on rattan pole exports, buyers presented their furniture designs to PTMC directly, to be manufactured in the Philippines. While inexperienced in furniture manufacturing, Streegan faced the challenge. The company's first factory was an 800-square-meter bamboo shack with a nipa roof, dirt floor and no lighting – except for gas mantle lamps and blowtorches in place of boilers. Production began in January 1976 and by April, PTMC had delivered its first shipment. Eventually, Streegan bought out his partners and became the sole proprietor of Pacific Traders. His wife, Gorgonia, headed the quality control and finishing section. In 1985, PTMC received the 16th Golden Shell Award for Outstanding Performance in the export sector and in 1994, Streegan was named Export Champion of the South.

His daughter – Bernice Streegan Montenegro – joined the company in December 1985, upon graduating with a degree in Ricercatore in Architettura Industriale (Industrial Design) from the Politecnico Internazionale di Architettura e Design in Milan, Italy. Her designs have received recognition in many furniture and interior design magazines. Today, Bernice heads the company's design team and is largely responsible for the company's product research and development.

Expansion of the business meant setting up affiliates to complement PTMC. In 1986, Worldmark Furniture Industries Inc. was established to produce a wide range of furniture, using a combination of wood, rattan, wrought iron, wicker and veneer. The wood division, set up in 1989, completed its furniture line – making the company less susceptible to the volatility of the supply of rattan poles. In 1990, PTMC's veneer production was spun off as Magellan Veneer Corporation – dedicated to making decorative veneer. A new 1,000-square-meter factory was built in 1993, equipped with modern, state-of-the-art machinery to boost its capability to include decorative veneer for wall and door panels and tabletops. Magellan Veneer Corporation's retail affiliate is Borders – headed by Streegan's daughter Alice Streegan Cruz. Located in Makati City, Borders was launched in 1996 to address the furniture needs of a largely high-end Philippine market.

Hugo and Gorgonia Streegan in 1998, Pacific Traders & Manufacturing Corp.'s 25th anniversary.

PTMC remains one of the largest furniture manufacturers and exporters in the Philippines. Management of the company is now held by the second generation, with Hugo's son Charles Streegan as President. PTMC remains committed to its reputation of producing high-quality classic and contemporary furniture, reflecting the company's philosophy of showcasing the beauty of Filipino design and craftsmanship to the world.

basquet

MATERIALS: rattan poles and slats with leather binding
SIZE: chair H 78.7 x W 71.1 x D 81.3 cm;
ottoman H 43.2 x W 63.5 x D 63.5 cm
DESIGNER: eileen cohen
MANUFACTURER: pacific traders & manufacturing corp.
CLIENT: Jovel
YEAR: 1983

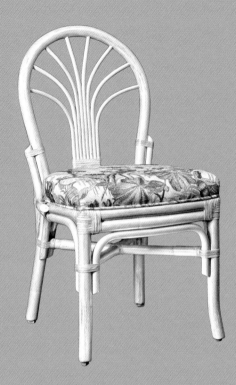

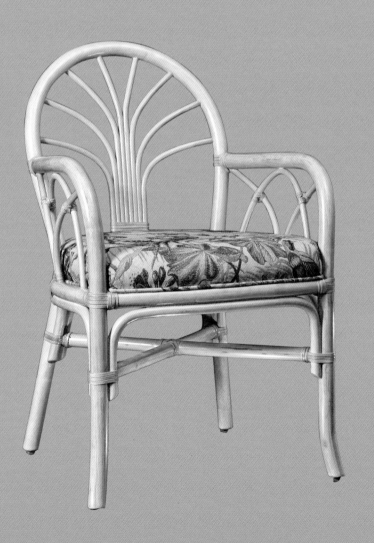

model 5505 arm chair and 5500 side chair

MATERIALS: rattan frame and leather wrappings
for the joints
DESIGNER: shelby williams in collaboration with
eduardo c. alegrado
MANUFACTURER: alenter cane corporation
CLIENT: shelby williams
YEAR: 1978

The models 5505 arm chair and 5500 side chair are light, airy
and happy. The simplicity of the design – simple flowing lines
for the main frames, good lumbar support for the back, and
seats that have good pitch to allow comfortable seating –
makes the chairs easy to adapt to different environments.

MINDANAO RATTAN CORPORATION

Mindanao Rattan was one of the largest exporters of rattan poles in Cebu, together with Standard Rattan, Alenter Cane, Norkis Trading and Pacific Traders & Manufacturing Corp. The company started exporting rattan poles to U.S. and European markets in the 1960s – Spain being their largest market – until the 1970s. The ban on the export of rattan poles in 1976 made Mindanao Rattan's entry into furniture manufacturing a matter of survival. And with the invaluable help and experience of Guillermo Figueroa, they set up their first factory.

From 1979 to 1986, rattan furniture was the top choice of the European market. This demand contributed to a booming business, which saw Mindanao Rattan employ as many as 2,500 workers in its factories. By 1986, the scarcity of rattan poles encouraged Mindanao Rattan to diversify into wood and mixed media furniture – much like the other furniture manufacturers in Cebu.

Mindanao Rattan remained one of the Philippine's largest furniture exporters until the worldwide recession in 1992. Unable to sustain rising operational expenses with falling sales, Mindanao Rattan closed shop and reincarnated into a smaller, leaner and more focused entity – Reunion Furnishings Inc.

ALENTER CANE CORPORATION

In 1978, the Philippine government's thrust to increase exports – in order to shore up the country's dwindling dollar reserves – sent the Board of Investments (BOI) to the countryside. The BOI organized seminars headed by a team of resource speakers from the Central Bank of the Philippines, Bureau of Customs, the Department of Finance and other government agencies, and aimed at encouraging small and medium-sized businesses to engage in the business of exports.

Brothers Arcadio and Eduardo Alegrado were among those who responded to the call. They set up a company that same year, which they registered as Alenter Cane Corporation, for the purpose of manufacturing and exporting rattan furniture. Demand for Philippine-made handicrafts, including rattan and *buri* furniture, was on the rise.

The rattan pole is a material which can be bent and twisted into different shapes with the application of heat. Ideally, the heat source is steam – so the rattan material does not become scorched. But heat from a kerosene-fired blowtorch will also suffice, as expert manipulation minimizes scorching and the scorched area, if any, can be scraped away. Furthermore, the bent rattan parts can easily be put together, ideally with metal screws driven in with an electric screwdriver, although the same job can also be accomplished with a hammer and nails.

As the creation of rattan furniture does not require intensive capital or sophisticated tools and equipment, it is easy to see why the beginning of this industry was really "the backyard". At that time, all an entrepreneur desirous of opening a rattan furniture factory had to do was gather backyard rattan furniture makers together under one roof, provide them with raw materials, workbenches, proper tools, workable designs, a working system and quality control systems, and he was soon in business.

But Alenter did more than that. It innovated on quality-improving and cost-saving production systems, searched for better materials and developed new designs and applications. Alenter also responded to its customers' need for timely deliveries and improved employee morale through better pay and good working conditions. More importantly, Alenter walked the extra mile for its clients.

Today, 32 years later, Alenter remains just as vibrant under a new name – Ambiente Designs International Inc. Its products continue to be found in some of the best hotels and resorts in the world.

Alenter Cane rattan
poles stockyard and
warehouse floor

OTHER EARLY PLAYERS

INTERIOR CRAFTS OF THE ISLANDS

Interior designer Betty Cobonpue scoured factories and showrooms for furniture to be incorporated into her designs. Frustrated at the unavailability of furniture and accessories in line with her concepts, she began to manufacture what she needed on a very small scale. Backyard production was a convenient option for Cobonpue, who – like most multi-tasking mothers – juggled children, home and husband with work. Cobonpue opened Interior Crafts of the Islands in 1972. As her children grew, so did her business, and she soon found herself lured to the export market.

In the 1970s export was strongly encouraged by the Philippine government, who pushed local industries to earn much-needed U.S. dollars to support the government's insatiable demand for foreign currency. The furniture industry was at the forefront of new non-traditional export potentials and the government dangled many incentives for companies to participate. Export fairs were organized by the Center

lotus side chairs >

MATERIAL: laminated rattan veins
SIZE: H 92 x W 48 x D 66 cm
DESIGNER: betty cobonpue
STYLISTIC VARIATIONS: side chair, club chair, sofa, dining table
MANUFACTURER: interior crafts of the islands inc.
YEAR: 1980s

The Lotus Side Chairs appear soft and graceful in their solidity.

biedermeier scroll
loveseat

MATERIAL: laminated rattan
SIZE: H 84 x W 183 x D 74 cm
DESIGNER: betty cobonpue
STYLISTIC VARIATIONS: sofa
MANUFACTURER: interior crafts of the islands inc.
YEAR: 1980s

Inspired by the defined clean lines and ornamentation of
the Biedermeier era, this piece is elegant and functional in
its simplicity.

for International Trade Expositions and Missions (CITEM), tapping members of the Chamber of Furniture Industries of the Philippines (CFIP) to take part in the shows.

Interior Crafts of the Islands was invited by the then-Cebu chapter of the CFIP to join the Manila exhibition. It was to be Cobonpue's first show and she knew she needed to make an impression, using a design never seen before. Like many Filipinos raised in the Catholic faith, Cobonpue turned to prayer for inspiration and got her answer – she was going to make ribbons. Using new techniques for rattan, she fashioned raised rattan ribbons. Incorporated as elements of her furniture, they added dimension and texture to her pieces. This design innovation made a big impact and elevated Interior Crafts of the Islands into the mainstream of furniture exporting.

Cobonpue's son Kenneth joined the company in 1996, upon returning home with a degree in Industrial Design from the Pratt Institute in New York. After graduation, he

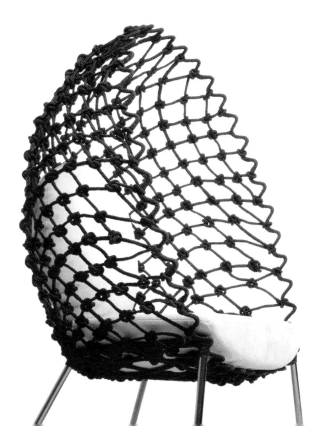

Dragnet Chair designed by Kenneth Cobonpue, 2005.

had apprenticed for a leather and wood workshop near Florence, Italy and pursued further studies in Furniture Marketing and Production in Reutlingen, Germany. He has since taken over the business and now manages the company, moving it towards his brand – Kenneth Cobonpue – positioned to bring modern and innovative design, using organic materials, to today's contemporary lifestyle.

CASTILEX INDUSTRIAL CORPORATION

Three former Philippine Air Force officers – Colonel Quirico Gamallo, Guido Castillo and Pat Casquejo – founded Castilex Industrial Corporation in 1974. The company was engaged in export trading of handicrafts and seashells, with Pier 1 Imports as one of its major clients.

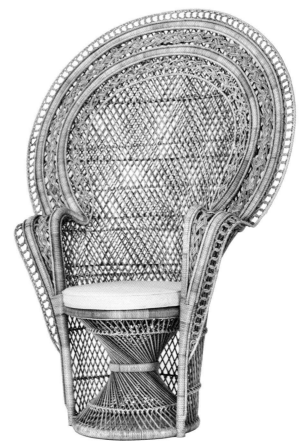

Not long after Castilex was created, Castillo and Casquejo sold their shares to Antonio Veloso. In 1977 Gamallo also sold his remaining shares to Veloso, who invited his good friend Augustin Climaco to spearhead the operations of Castilex Industrial Corporation. During Climaco's time, from the late 1970s to the early 80s, Castilex became the largest supplier of *buri* furniture to the U.S. – primarily because of Pier 1 Imports.

The demand for *buri* fiber eventually decreased in the mid-1980s with the rise of the more appealing, sturdy and flexible rattan. Castilex shifted production and tried very hard to crack the niche of the major rattan buyers, but was only mildly successful – despite the Golden Rattan Era in Cebu. At that time up to the early 1990s, the company was focused on selling rattan furniture largely to the European market.

Upon the passing of Climaco in 1993, Veloso bought Climaco's shares from his heirs. Antonio R. Veloso, Sr. then took the reins of Castilex as CEO, with his son Michael J. Veloso as President. He decided to completely expand the company's product line

A sketch of a party chair by Florentino Atillo III on a piece of tissue paper for Allied Stores in 1976.

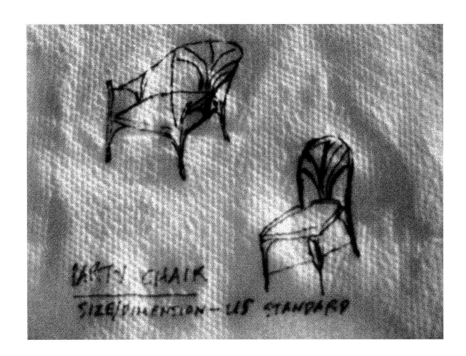

from mostly rattan furniture, to wooden furniture with mixed media. As a result, Castilex is now one of the largest and most reliable suppliers of rattan and wooden furniture to the U.S.

ATILLO MANUFACTURING CORPORATION

Florentino Atillo III was born into furniture. As the son of industry pioneer Florentino Rallos Atillo, he learned the business of making furniture early in life working in the family factory at the age of 17 and taking over from his late father at the age of 19. He married in 1972, and with his wife Irma soon left the company to start a new business from the ground up. They worked out of their first home in P. del Rosario St., sourcing local materials from Butuan, then selling rattan, plywood and other products to furniture manufacturers in Cebu, building the capital needed to open their own factory.

By 1976 they established Atillo Manufacturing Corporation (AMANCOR) at a one-hectare property in Guizo, Mandaue, producing only rattan furniture. AMANCOR also sold *buri* furniture sourced from different suppliers. The following year, 1977, the first-ever large volume shipment from Cebu was completed by AMANCOR for Pier 1 Imports. Seventy-eight 40-foot containers provided by Filsov Lines were filled with rattan lounge chairs and *buri* étagère sets of four. Cebu was not prepared to ship so many 40-foot containers at one time and there were no trucks or trailers to transport these steel containers to the factory. Neither were there cranes at the pier to handle all 78 containers from ship to pier and back again, accustomed as they were to mostly smaller knockdown crates and single-container shipments.

Irma recalls trucking all the chairs and étagère from the factory to the pier, unloading them by hand and filling the containers while they sat stacked on the ship, beginning from the topmost and working downwards slowly until they were all filled. This backbreaking work went on for hours and remains an experience and source of satisfaction that today's success and plenty cannot blur.

Construction of the AMANCOR factory was based on Florentino III's masterplan and layout. Built phase by phase as business progressed, it was completed in 1980. The business thrived and in 1988, Florentino III International Inc. (F3) was developed to diversify the company's interests to include furniture crafted from wood, leather, stone, metal, cast, fiberglass and weaves.

Expanding its reach to its main market in the U.S., F3 developed subsidiaries in California (F3 USA) and Arkansas (F3 Arkansas). Instead of building new factories, F3 forged partnerships with 24 other independent companies, choosing to outsource their products instead of manufacturing items themselves. The father and daughter team of Florentino III and Melissa Atillo – a graduate of Fashion Institute of Design & Merchandising Los Angeles – conceptualized the designs, while the fully contracted factories executed the plans to the company's standards. Over the years, cost issues compelled F3 to move much of their production requirements to China. Melissa, however, is currently working to move production back to Cebu – where the company began.

Florentino III and his wife Irma were grateful for the gains their business achieved. On February 25, 2000 – the millennium year and a profitable peak for the company – F3 hosted an appreciation dinner at Shangri-La's Mactan Resort and Spa, inviting everyone who had been involved in the business, from company officers and staff, to bankers, suppliers and customers. Presidents, COOs and other executives flew in from different parts of the world to share the celebrations. It was a time to honor relationships and friendships, the ties that continue to bind the people behind the business.

In 2001, F3 received the second Presidential Award from President Gloria Macapagal Arroyo, for achieving the highest export gross sales in furniture in the Philippines.

GAMALLOSONS

In 1977, after Philippine Air Force retired Colonel Quiric Gamallo left Castilex, he incorporated Gamallosons – shipping exclusively to Pier 1 Imports. In 1980, he created Mandaue Galleon Trade, and both companies went on to play a large part in the *buri* furniture and handicraft trade.

Less than a decade later, Othello Gamallo, the eldest child in a brood of seven, opened the metal working section of Gamallosons. He is one of the first, if not the first, to commercialize metal furniture manufacturing in Cebu. Gamallosons has since become one of the leading metal furniture exporters of Cebu.

Abaca is a species of banana common in the Philippines.

The *abaca* fiber is extracted from the stalk of the plant. There are two most commonly used methods of *abaca* fiber extraction, namely hand stripping and spindle stripping.

growth
and
expansion

n the midst of the boom in furniture export, which began in the 1980s and lasted until the first few years of the 21st century, industry development and expansion inevitably led to the arrival of new factories and new entrepreneurs.

Many in the furniture industry attribute a turning point in its history to when Paul Maitland-Smith – an antique dealer and furniture manufacturer based in Hong Kong – began sourcing furniture and eventually opened his own furniture factory in Cebu in 1982.

Maitland-Smith raised a new awareness for working with wood in styles and ways which were simply different to what everyone else was doing. After Maitland-Smith's arrival, Cebu saw more factories specializing in stone, iron, fiberglass and synthetic furniture being built. And Cebu began to attract many buyers from all over the world who no longer associated the industry with rattan alone.

leather-wrapped > book cocktail table

MATERIALS: leather inlay on solid mahogany with gilded tooling on book names and authors
SIZE: H 42.5 x W 91.4 x D 73.3 cm
DESIGNER: paul maitland-smith
MANUFACTURER: maitland-smith
YEAR: 1986

Inspired by a 19th century box in the form of books, this cocktail table is an iconic piece of the Maitland-Smith leather inlayed furniture era, and still one of the pieces most in demand. The combined finishes give the appearance of a stack of oversize antique books, with the book "spines" sliding open to reveal drawers lined in watermarked paper made in England.

MAITLAND-SMITH CEBU INC. – THE COMPANY

Maitland-Smith Limited was founded in Hong Kong in 1979 to make fine quality furniture and accessories. The company originally manufactured in Hong Kong, but due to the scarcity of skilled local workers, production was relocated to the Philippines.

The first factory, Maitland-Smith Philippines Inc. (MSPI) – located in Mandaue City, Cebu – opened in 1982. Within six years of operation, MSPI had expanded and produced a wide variety of premium products made from wood, shagreen, stone, shell and rattan.

As the company's business grew, further facilities were needed and in June 1988, a major factory – now known as Maitland-Smith Cebu Inc. – was built at the Mactan Export Processing Zone (since renamed Mactan Economic Zone) in Cebu. In 2006 the workforce peaked at 5,300 employees. Today's workforce is lower, as demand for high-quality home furnishing waned during the global economic crisis.

mother of pearl >
shell dish

MATERIALS: silver plated cast brass,
natural mother of pearl shell
SIZE: H 12.7 x W 17.8 x D 20.3 cm
FINISH: silver plating with light natural antique hue
DESIGNER: pride sasser
MANUFACTURER: maitland-smith
YEAR: 1997

This dish is inspired by the natural and timeless beauty of shells.

At present, the Cebu operations of Maitland-Smith, housed in a 570,000-square-foot facility, consist of four manufacturing plants and a Regional Operating Headquarters. Production includes manufacturing of wood furniture, brassware, lighting, accessories and metal furniture. In addition, the facility provides support services such as product design, development and engineering, sales support, sourcing and procurement, human resources, business planning and production control, finance and information technology.

Maitland-Smith is known for its fine foundry/metal finished goods, made using the lost wax process – whereby wax carvings are faithfully translated into metal. All wood furniture products exhibit highly-regarded and technical furniture craft inlay processes, such as marquetry and parquetry. Lamps and accessories have intricate and distinct designs, often an assembly of high-quality materials and components. And while the vast majority of Maitland-Smith's output is shipped to U.S. customers, the facility also supplies items to customers in Asia and the Middle East.

MAITLAND-SMITH MAKES A DIFFERENCE

Paul Maitland-Smith was an English cabinet maker, whose business involved restoring and selling English antique furniture, as well as crafting antique reproductions. Learning from his grandfather – acquiring the eye and the sense that can only belong to one of a line of generations before him – he began collecting antiques from an early age. Furniture was in his blood and his vision was born from exposure to centuries of tradition.

Unhappy with the high cost of labor in England, he traveled around the world in 1973, searching for a new place for his workshop. For some strange reason – and to some regret – he never made it to the Philippines at that time. He set up shop in Seoul, South Korea, working with local Korean manufacturers. But by 1978, wages in Korea had gone up and he moved his manufacturing to Hong Kong and China. And while Hong Kong was producing excellent work in lacquer, porcelain and coromandel, woodwork and veneer were lacking.

An Englishman by the name of Albert Roberts offered to make Maitland-Smith chairs out of a factory in Manila. By 1979, Maitland-Smith ended his business in Korea and commissioned Philippine company Grandwood Furniture to manufacture wooden case goods and chairs. It was his first venture in the Philippines.

While in Hong Kong in 1980, Maitland-Smith chanced upon jewelry boxes and objects with stone inlay. Upon enquiry, he discovered they were made in Cebu. Until then he had never heard of Cebu and a quick call to Roberts – plus a gracious offer to take him to the island – soon found him on a trip of discovery, as he met potential manufacturers in Cebu. Maitland-Smith's first endeavor involved stone and shell inlay on wood, teaching his contractors manufacturing techniques which improved the quality of their work and kept the inlay secure.

Maitland-Smith then opened his first manufacturing plant in Cebu in 1982, converting an old chicken farm into a factory. Shortly after, he bought an existing rattan furniture factory in Mandaue City from the Gothong family.

Maitland-Smith's entry into the local manufacturing industry opened doors to other foreign nationals, changing the environment within which the industry operated. His pioneering efforts were initially looked on as a threat to the existing producers, competition to a set of players in a then immature industry. However, Maitland-Smith's presence actually gave birth to many new businesses, teaching techniques and a refinement of skills – exposing the locals to a different market.

Maitland-Smith had great success in combining rattan and metal. Together with his designers – among them Winsor White, who cleverly executed his concept and Pride Sasser and Howard Shattuck, who perfected the design and attachment techniques – rattan with metal went on to be a big hit in the market. Maitland-Smith introduced the manufacture of leather-wrapped furniture and the use of shagreen. Together with sub-contractors, he developed techniques in fine brass castings. He also produced pottery, worked with stone and shell and made solid wood furniture accentuated by top-quality carvings. Except for porcelain and coromandel, he tried to do many things in Cebu, making use of raw talent and further refining craftsmen's skills. When it came to manufacturing, a large part of the company's growth was also helped by its partnership with Tony Yu and his company CCIC.

Recognizing the enormity of the American market, Maitland-Smith forged a partnership with Henredon in 1981 – selling 30 percent of his company in the deal – to distribute his furniture exclusively to the U.S.. The partnership thrived through the years, with Henredon maintaining a "hands-off" policy over Maitland-Smith's operations. Eventually, in 1994, Maitland-Smith left. A year later, he relocated to India, then to Vietnam and started again, creating the company Theodore and Alexander. Maitland-Smith took with him a large number of talented Filipino workers to get his new operations up and running as effortlessly as possible, doing more or less the same as he had done in Cebu.

Maitland-Smith claims he is now retired, but continues to be prolifically creative. He says, "If I had to live my life all over again, I would return to Cebu and start from there. You can do almost anything in Cebu". He now lives in Thailand with his Filipino wife and returns to Cebu from time to time.

A GREAT SUCCESS

From the mid-1980s, Cebu was at the center of the furniture universe and known as a hot-spot for creative design and superior craftsmanship. Buyers and investors came to Cebu not only for the furniture, but also for the lifestyle Cebu had to offer. Visitors looked forward to an afternoon at the beach, mulling over selections made at the showroom in the morning, and discussing business over cold drinks and fresh seafood by the seaside before dusk. Foreign nationals who chose to relocate and set up shop in Cebu found a way of life unattainable in their home countries, enjoying luxuries they could not otherwise afford. Many of them went on to marry Filipino wives, making their immersion in local culture and society complete.

Foreign designers, buyers, and manufacturers claim the Cebuano workforce is ideal – possessing a strong design sense and an innate artistic aesthetic not found elsewhere in Asia. Creativity comes naturally and craftsmanship is intrinsic, enabling Cebuanos to consistently produce some of the finest hand carvings and inlay work in the world. Filipinos have been observed to be emotionally involved in their work, bringing an integrity which keeps them focused on producing a beautiful final product, relishing a sense of pride at having done a marvelous job. They are masters of their hands and have a good eye for color. And while these traits are qualities of great craftsmen, they can work against a production line whose thrust is quantity over quality.

Cebu is the perfect environment for high-end, good-quality fine furniture production, required to be finished by hand in limited quantities. Skilled manpower is readily available, infrastructure to support the furniture industry is already in place and a vast network of capable third-party contractors exists. It is the general impression of foreign buyers and designers that the local manufacturers – including their individual workers – value being the best, over being the biggest. The local manufacturers and craftsmen take those extra few minutes to get things done just right and devote a

Opposite page: Cebu's craftsmen are known to have an eye for detail and are masters of their hands. Some of these master craftsmen have been in the industry for over 40 years.

Far left. Cebuano craftsmen produce high-end and quality furniture by hand. Even though pieces are handmade, these craftsmen can still beat mass production lines whose thrust is quantity over quality.

Left: Lacquer is applied on a furniture piece made of rattan peel.

great deal of thought to making a chair more graceful, putting customer satisfaction above profit.

Those who recognize the real value of the people and what Cebu has to offer have built their factories and stayed.

COSONSA MANUFACTURING, INC.

Cosonsa Manufacturing, Inc. opened its facilities in Cebu in 1995, producing metal sculptures, lamps and furniture. Its owner and lead designer, Pride Sasser, first came to Cebu to work with Paul Maitland-Smith. At Maitland-Smith for more than eight years, Sasser immersed himself in his boss's prolific accomplishments. Impressed with the passion and pride Cebuanos put into their work, he decided to stay after Maitland-Smith left Cebu. A native of North Carolina, U.S., with a Fine Arts (major in Sculpture) degree tucked under his belt, Sasser set out to build a business to cater to the U.S. luxury market. His pieces speak of old money. Designing with understated elegance, in classic styles that never go out of fashion, Sasser fuses indigenous materials with silver and applies techniques formerly only used in the making of fine jewelry.

bamboo collection >

MATERIALS: bamboo and mahogany
FINISH: ebonized
DESIGNER: pride sasser
MANUFACTURER: cosonsa manufacturing, inc.
YEAR: 2000

The Bamboo Collection is a reinterpretation of Modern Art by using unusual and locally available materials to suit the American and European markets.

obelisk

MATERIALS: aluminum frame wrapped in DEDON Fiber
SIZE: stacked obelisk H 244 x Dia. 80 cm; medium lounge chair
H 66 x Dia. 80 cm; small lounge chair H 66 x Dia. 72 cm; table
H 57 x Dia. 56 cm
DESIGNER: frank ligthart
MANUFACTURER: DEDON
YEAR: 2004

The Obelisk is a seven-piece sculpture that, when taken apart,
clearly reveals the precisely thought-out concept behind the
art. It is a powerful, modular and surprisingly versatile work
that stands out in any setting.

DEDON

Bobby Dekeyser retired from professional football as a goalkeeper of *Bayern Munich* at the age of 26, after suffering a bad injury. His accident may have ended one career, but it opened the door of opportunity for another, which would eventually place him and his work a cut above the rest. Dekeyser dreamed of creating an outdoor living room, using weatherproof furniture that could withstand the sun, rain and extreme temperatures, while remaining colorfast and sturdy. He founded DEDON in 1990 and went in search of the right idea.

Dekeyser found wicker furniture while attending a furniture trade fair in the Philippines, inspiring him to combine his family's wealth of experience in plastics with the centuries-old art of weaving. Using his inherited decades of knowledge in plastics and his family's manufacturing plant specializing in high-quality synthetics, he developed a new type of fiber – one that was washable, extremely easy to clean and 100 percent recyclable, plus resistant to sunlight, salt water and both high and low temperatures.

In collaboration with Agustin Climaco of Castilex Industrial Corporation, Dekeyser experimented with various structural materials – beginning with rattan. Together they produced a prototype which proved to be too heavy, unwieldy and bulky, which was also unable to be guaranteed to withstand extreme weather in extended periods. Further research and product development ultimately led to the use of aluminum – the backbone of DEDON furniture today.

The seven pieces in this set fit together to form an obelisk for which the collection is named.

Dekeyser worked with weavers from the Philippines, China, Thailand and Indonesia. In the end, he chose to settle in Cebu – following the conclusion that the exceptional quality of workmanship negated the significantly higher costs of production. The company considers Cebu's weavers to be among the best in the world, crediting much of its products' beauty to the skill and dedication of its employees.

Dekeyser first met with Castilex in 1992. By 1993, Castilex became DEDON's first manufacturer of outdoor furniture, using a combination of rattan and DEDON Fiber. With the desire to be totally responsible and in control of its products, DEDON opened its first factory in Cebu in 2000. The company developed an all-encompassing corporate philosophy, which has resulted in high productivity, a healthy and happy workforce and a business which is an asset to both the community and the Philippines as a country.

DEDON's current CEO/Managing Partner, Hervé Lampert, responsible for Cebu operations from 2000 to 2010, immersed himself in the company culture and local way of life. He focused on creating a relationship with employees which bred mutual respect, espousing a belief that the company's founder, Bobby Dekeyser, lives by, "Only a satisfied employee can create a comfortable chair". Today, Hervé's brother, Vince Lampert, leads the Cebu operations, continuing Bobby Dekeyser's quest for DEDON to reach greater heights and accomplish his vision – "To create the most desirable company in the world".

The company is able to stay on top of its game by always being ahead in design, commissioning international designers to create lifestyle concepts unique to DEDON. It recognizes the design collections of Richard Frinier and Frank Ligthart as breakthroughs, which took DEDON in the direction it is in today. Lately, other world-class designers including Philippe Starck, Jean-Marie Massaud and Toan Nguyen, have also joined the DEDON design crew. DEDON is helping to put Cebu on a different map, one that brings to mind exclusivity, luxury and uncompromising quality.

DRIVEN BY DESIGN

Changing trends and a maturing industry recognized the importance of design and designers to the continued growth and success of Cebu's furniture business. For the most part of the industry's existence, foreign designers and their designs dictated which products would sell and therefore what would be manufactured. The emergence of Cebuano designers, educated in the best design schools in the U.S. and Europe and trained by top American and European designers, saw companies bucking tradition. Design innovations using organic indigenous materials began to appear, introducing both new techniques and applications.

In 1997, seven young designers, mavericks of their time, founded the Cebu Furniture Designers Guild. Maria Luisa delos Santos, Bernice Montenegro, Kenneth Cobonpue, Corito Escario Yu, Debbie Palao, Ramon Castellanos and Rene Ybañez came together to propagate their fold and elevate their lot, by linking with other professional design groups abroad to exchange ideas through seminars and information transfer. Their objective was to learn and work in conjunction with the Cebu Furniture Industries Foundation (CFIF). Unfortunately, the guild was short-lived, constantly beleaguered by lack of funds and support.

The Cebu Design Education Foundation (CDEF) emerged in 2009, formed by a core group of design professionals and educators, organized mainly to support sustainable development of design disciplines through design education. While it has yet to make its mark on the furniture industry, it has taken the first step by ensuring the continued personal growth of Cebu designers.

Through the lobbying of some of its members, an industrial design course at the University of the Philippines Cebu campus is finally being offered. Kenneth Cobonpue is one of the thesis advisers, taking on the role of teacher, sharing what he has learned

Below: A *capiz* shell floor lamp (with detail) designed by Val Padilla, 2010.

and opening young students' eyes to what is possible. He recognizes the dearth of up-and-coming designers and has personally taken responsibility to help fill the void through education.

Independent American designers continue to work in Cebu, claiming a distinct knowledge of what will sell in the U.S. market to be their advantage over their Filipino counterparts. They cite the lack of exposure of many local designers to market trends and different lifestyles as shortcomings, which can only be corrected by constant travel.

Regrettably, opportunities for travel do not come often to those who cannot afford it. Filipino designers have to content themselves with working with foreigners and learning as they go along, severely limiting their potential. It is expected that the CDEF will step in as it introduces new programs envisioned to attract the best and the brightest designers from different parts of the globe.

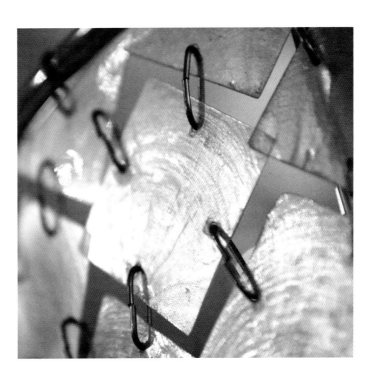

STAGING A REVOLUTION

The year 1992 witnessed the start of a revolution. Mixed media arrived on the scene, with producers displaying new and interesting ways to combine rattan, split rattan core, wood, stone, shell, metal, leather, marble and other materials. Manufacturers known for rattan showed items without any rattan at all, using a mix of *lauan* (Philippine mahogany), wrought iron, rattan peel, coconut bark and cocowood. Sea grass, animal skins, palms and reeds – considered exotic materials – were also featured. Emphasis was on the use of indigenous materials fused ingeniously, in an unusual and distinctive manner, making Philippine design unique. Design Today called it "a synthesis of Eastern and Western influences", referring to centuries of Spanish colonization and strong American ties as the Philippines' most significant Western persuasions.

console mosaic table

MATERIALS: natural fossilized stones and wrought iron
FINISH: smooth (stone top), rust (base)
DESIGNER: paola navone
STYLISTIC VARIATIONS: mural and dining table
MANUFACTURER: raphael legacy designs, inc.
YEAR: 1995

The challenge for Paula Navone was to create a Filipino idiom for a mosaic furniture piece without bringing in too many mosaic elements from her native Italy. The result is an understated, monochromatic floral and scroll design for the mosaic console table, set on a textured wrought-iron base, with legs topped by domes reminiscent of minarets. The piece is Oriental with subtle hints of European influence. It may be used for its typical purpose, or treated as a piece of art – as it is a statement in itself.

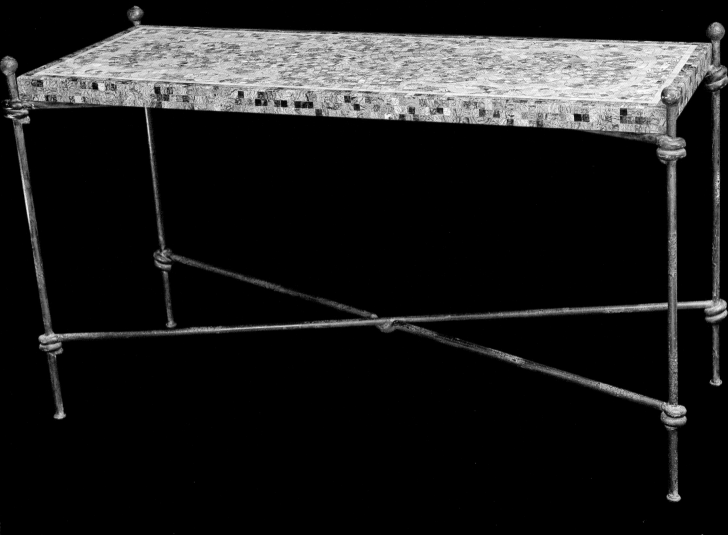

MOSAIC

Raphael Legacy Design Inc., like most of its industry counterparts in Cebu, started its business producing high-end rattan furniture – largely for the Japanese market. Established in 1987 by Charles Belleza and Seth Tugonon, 100 percent of its rattan requirements were sourced from Mindanao. The looming shortage of rattan poles made it necessary for the company to diversify into stonecraft, combining stone and iron in its furniture and accessories. But stonecraft was replicated in several other factories; it was not unique. Belleza knew he needed a new product, something original and innovative, for his company to truly succeed. He searched for inspiration and on a trip to Venice, Italy, he found it in the mosaic work at St. Mark's Basilica and in the patterns on the pavement of the Piazza San Marco. Years of research and experimentation paid off and by 1994, the Philippine Bureau of Patents, Trademarks and Technology Transfer awarded Raphael Legacy Design Inc. a utility patent for its line of mosaic products, recognizing its pioneering efforts in the country.

Detail of Tuscan Coffee Table by Alain Nejar for Raphael Legacy Designs Inc., 2005. Made of fossilized stones, this table is a marriage between traditional designs and modern materials to create a refreshing piece suited for the outdoors.

The mosaic process involves cutting stone by machine, then putting pieces together by hand, creating works akin to art. Belleza's technique has achieved a sophistication through the years, enabling him to come up with what he calls micro-mosaic – using tiny pieces of stone painstakingly laid out by hand. Belleza continues to innovate, giving serious thought to branding his work in the not-so-distant future.

NATURE'S LEGACY IS GREEN

Nature's Legacy has taken the high road, the road less traveled, by embracing a philosophy many companies pay little attention but lip service to. The company has a healthy respect for the environment, creating Naturescast® – an innovative line of products using dry leaves, dead twigs and fallen bark as primary materials to manufacture earth-friendly, attractive and functional furniture and accessories.

Pedro Herrera Delantar Jr., together with his wife Catherine, founded the company in December 1996. They form a working team using Cathy's vision and Pete's precision to direct the company forward and achieve their objectives. Delantar carries with him years of working in the furniture industry and a familiarity with rattan and its success. He originally started his business with rattan, riding the wave many other manufacturers were on, from 1986 to 1995. But Delantar was an inventor, a man with a strong pioneering spirit, who soon came to realize rattan would not take him towards his dream for his family. He abandoned rattan and went with his first original process – stonecast. The process involved using natural crushed stone, dry-stamped by hand into a mold, simulating how the earth made limestone.

The finished product possessed the same physical and aesthetic qualities as cut limestone, but was more lightweight and durable. It enjoyed wide acceptability in

the export market and it was not long before the process was copied. Delantar faced stiff competition from people who had not invested in research and development. He fought – and continues to fight – a legal battle with those who adopted the methods which he considers rightfully belong to his company. Despite the setback, Delantar could not stop. He watched his profits erode from price wars and litigation expenses, so he moved on and launched Naturescast® in 2004 with renewed enthusiasm.

The company continues to manufacture castings using materials from nature, stonecast and Marmorcast, but Naturescast® is their anchor. The company's future is hitched on Pete and Cathy's advocacy for environmental preservation and social progress, positively transforming lives in the community by providing livelihood and spreading an environmental awareness to protect generations to come.

< anja collection

MATERIALS: Naturescast® (agro-forest waste), carb
(-certified) plywood
FINISH: natural color of Naturescast®, two-tone
DESIGNER: giovanne buzon
MANUFACTURER: nature's legacy eximport, inc.
YEAR: 2010

Inspired by geometric shapes and forms, the Anja Collection is compact and functional modern – multi-purpose, multi-functional and eco-friendly.

designing
for the world

cebu furniture
global gallery

b&b united u. s. bo
italia kingdom asia
varya home maitland-
designs vinotti smith g
europe bonacina geo
mcguire hong kim
chelsea bernard kong nue
house christianson jo
australia robb & stucky
thomasville red a
furniture brown a
india mexico batuka s

macina pierantonio
middle
east
oggetti atelier'a
shelby williams
orsia design
dominican
republic
ge de elite st.barth brazil
haast
philippines
tienda
el habitats ethan
africa ito allen
te primitivo kish globe
tistica weylandts west
west
uth africa indies

The furniture pieces and accessories shown in the following pages of the Cebu Furniture Global Gallery (1970-2011) have been selected by the leading industry players as their landmark and best-selling works. These reflect the demands of the market and the prevalent styles of their time.

All works carry the mark of the high quality of craftsmanship and design, through the inspired use of indigenous materials that have seen remarkable evolutions with newer technologies, mixed media and design expertise.

Pages 92-93: Planter made of a rattan frame covered with scraped rattan weaving, designed by Fernando "Astik" Villarin, 2011.

Opposite page: Detail of *solehiya* weaving on Manhattan Hassock by Rene Ybañez for Obra Cebuana, 2010.

Right: Varona Chair designed by Val Padilla for Coast Pacific, 2010.

peacock chairs
[1]hong kong peacock chair
[2]princess peacock chair
[3]wing-back peacock chair

MATERIALS: *buri* midribs, rattan poles,
black plastic strips
DESIGNER: quirico f. gamallo
STYLISTIC VARIATIONS: the weaving can be single or double
weave and the base twisted or barrel
MANUFACTURER: gamallosons traders, inc.
YEAR: 1970

These timeless classics were inspired by the beauty and
grandeur of the peacock tail.

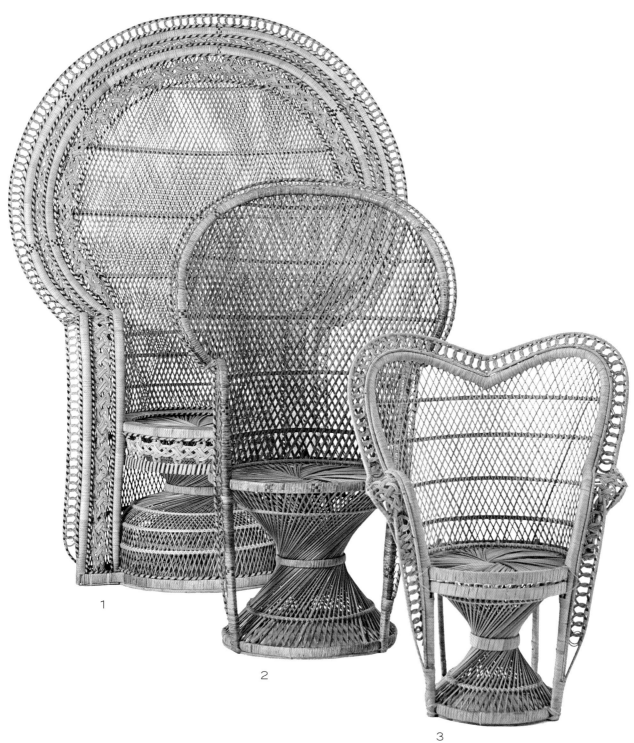

1

2

3

collezione basilan 1

MATERIALS: rattan
SIZE: side chair H 85 x W 46 x D 50 cm; bookshelf H 85 x W 171 x D 30 cm; small arm chair H 85 x W 65 x D 46 cm; table H 72 x W 180 x D 90 cm; sofa H 65 x W 200 x D 76 cm
DESIGNER: afra e tobia scarpa
MANUFACTURER: pacific traders & manufacturing corp.
CLIENT: b&b italia
YEAR: 1975

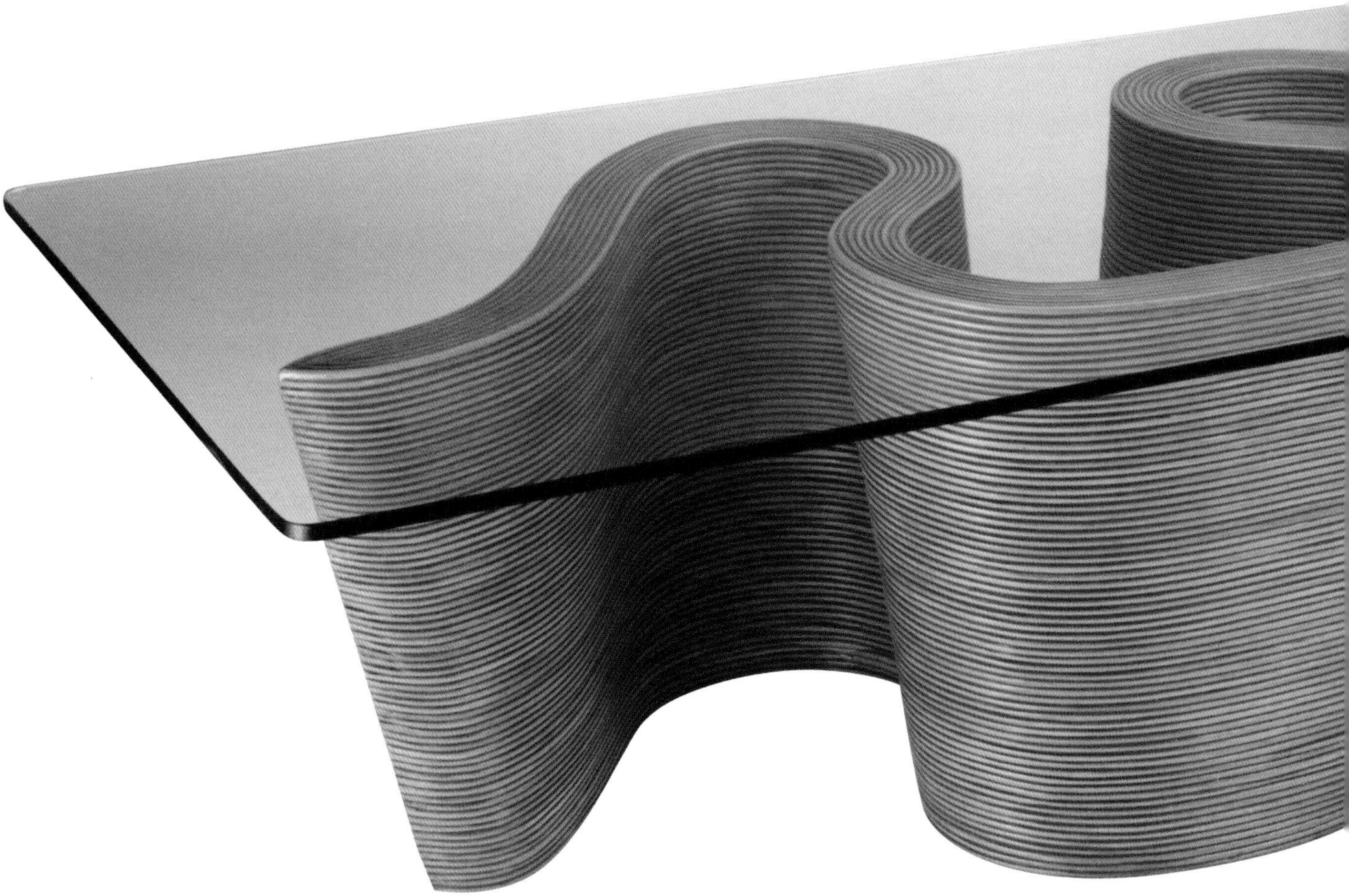

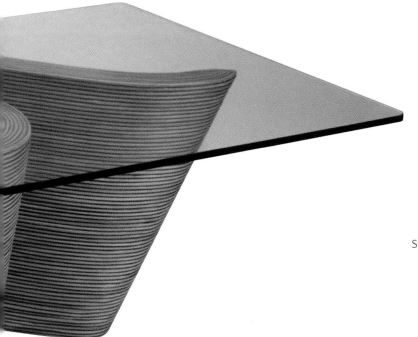

ribbon coffee table

MATERIAL: laminated rattan
SIZE: base H 38 x W 120 x D 45 cm; table top W 137 x D 61 cm
DESIGNER: betty cobonpue
STYLISTIC VARIATIONS: headboard, mirror frame,
end table, dresser
MANUFACTURER: interior crafts of the islands inc.
YEAR: 1980s

Inspired by a piece of silk ribbon dancing in a gentle breeze, the Ribbon Coffee Table gives the impression of graceful curves reminiscent of flowing water or soft fabric.

Wicker is hard woven fiber formed into a rigid material, usually used for baskets or furniture. Wicker is often made of material of plant origin, but plastic fibers are also used.

The milled core of rattan can be made into wicker. Other materials used can be any part of a plant or whole thicknesses of plants, as with willow switches. Bamboo and reed can also be used.

claudia
sofa

MATERIAL: 4 mm round wicker
SIZE: H 72.4 x W 232.4 x D 101.6 cm
DESIGNER: bernice montenegro
MANUFACTURER: pacific traders & manufacturing corp.
YEAR: 1985

Claudia was inspired by the desire to make something voluptuous, comfortable, and with smooth, round feeling areas all over. This classic set gives a feeling of boldness.

s-5

MATERIALS: wood and natural buffalo leather strips
SIZE: H 70 x W 67.9 x D 90 cm
DESIGNER: arch. antonio citterio
MANUFACTURER: pacific traders & manufacturing corp.
CLIENT: b&b italia
YEAR: 1985

Buffalo leather is typically tanned using traditional methods, called "brain tanning", which is an ancient practice used by Native Americans and several other tribal societies around the world. Brain tanning uses organic materials: brains, liver, bone marrow, castor or other natural oils, combined with wood smoke.

Other native tanning practices use the bark of a tree, such as oak. Smoking the hide at the end keeps the leather resistant to moths, preserves the fibers and allows the leather to stay soft and pliable even if it becomes wet. The result is a durable leather that is soft and breathable.

Cebu furniture makers have also experimented with the use of carabao leather.

s-4

MATERIALS: alder wood and natural buffalo leather strips
SIZE: H 70 x W 70 x D 64.9 cm
DESIGNER: arch. antonio citterio
MANUFACTURER: pacific traders & manufacturing corp.
CLIENT: b&b italia
YEAR: 1990

settee

MATERIALS: mahogany and rattan splits
SIZE: H 95.6 x W 152.4 x D 82.6 cm
DESIGNER: alain huin
MANUFACTURER: casa cebuana
YEAR: 1993

Inspired by French furniture design, the Settee is a simple but elegant piece that lends class and comfort.

The skin of rattan makes strand cane and cane webbing. These can be shaved in a machine to make rattan split as seen above.

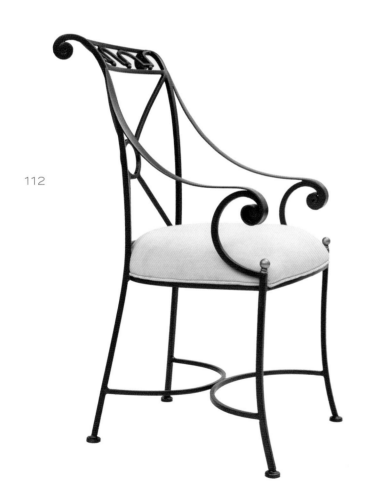

st. tropez
chair
table

MATERIALS: wrought iron, brass, glass, fossilized stone
SIZE: arm chair H 94 x W 63.5 x D 53.3 cm;
table H 53.4 x 71.1 x 71.1 cm
FINISH: gray pewter (metal base), gray (pastor stone top)
DESIGNER: leonard eisen
MANUFACTURER: mendco
YEAR: 1993

The St. Tropez Collection is a classic collection that responds to the demand for brass-accented iron and glass worked into stone. It was inspired by the combination of classic materials – old-fashioned Spanish iron scroll, fossil stone and beveled transparent glass in polished brass.

kandinsky coffee table

MATERIALS: solid wood gmelina, kalantas,
poplar burl, gmelina
SIZE: base H 39.4 x W 76.8 x D 79 cm;
table top W 100 x D 100 cm
FINISH: closed-pore matt; also comes in
duco yellow, red, blue
DESIGNER: maurice barilone
MANUFACTURER: cebu fil-veneer
CLIENTS: atelier'a
YEAR: 1995

The Kandinsky Coffee Table breaks the basic rule of furniture
making by using wood in abstract and unusual but beautiful
artistic shapes.

tortola sofa

MATERIALS: gmelina, open cane webbing
SIZE: H 116.2 x W 231.1 x D 101.6 cm
DESIGNER: rey g. ipong
MANUFACTURER: casa cebuana
YEAR: 1995

The Spanish style has always been considered a classic. The Tortola Sofa is no different with its intricate wood carving, size and open-cane weaving.

venetta egg-shaped coffee table

MATERIAL: flexible laminated coco round core
SIZE: small table H 25.4 x W 129.5 x D 91.4 cm;
large table H 30.5 x W 162.6 x D 121.9 cm
FINISH: white or black resin over the
round core's natural beige
DESIGNER: clayton tugonon
MANUFACTURER: classical geometry
CLIENTS: elite, weylandts
YEAR: 1995

While eating hard-boiled egg in a restaurant, the designer realized that the yolk of the egg would make a good and interesting table design.

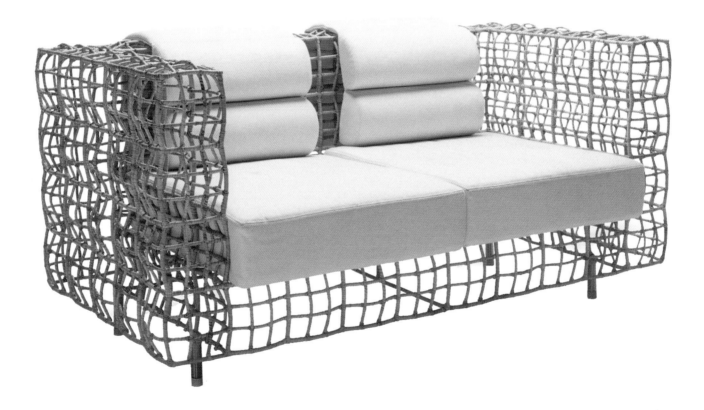

yin & yang
sofa
easy arm chair

MATERIALS: (indoor) rattan peel, rattan, steel, stainless steel;
(outdoor) polyethylene fiber, steel, stainless steel
SIZE: regular sofa H 71 x W 206 x D 77 cm;
regular easy arm chair H 71 x W 90.5 x D 77 cm
DESIGNER: kenneth cobonpue
STYLISTIC VARIATIONS: loveseat, L-sofa, coffee and end
tables, side chair, dining table, bed, night table, mirror frame
MANUFACTURER: interior crafts of the islands inc.
YEAR: 1997

As in the light and shadow created by a forest canopy on the
ground, there are opposing elements that come into play
within the Yin & Yang Collection.

The structure is very much a part of the form and disappears
within the layers created by rattan splits wrapped over a
frame of steel and wicker. It integrates material, function and
form. The result is both lightness and density, transparency
within the volume, a combination of the geometric and the
organic, and something square and something round.

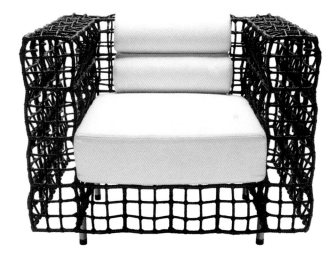

wing back chair

MATERIALS: rattan, caning, twill mats
SIZE: H 116.8 x W 81.3 x D 78.7 cm
FINISH: antique fruitwood
DESIGNER: winsor white
MANUFACTURER: mehitabel furniture inc.
CLIENTS: kim3, nuebo tienda
YEAR: 1998

Inspired by the traditional american winged-back arm chair.

pigalle

MATERIALS: (indoor) *abaca*, nylon twine, steel; (outdoor)
polyethylene fiber, nylon twine, steel
SIZE: H 75 x W 97 x D 100 cm
DESIGNER: kenneth cobonpue
STYLISTIC VARIATIONS: easy arm chair, loveseat,
dining table, bar stool
MANUFACTURER: interior crafts of the islands inc.
YEAR: 1999

A woman's body and its sensuous curves are turned into
sculptural pieces, calling to mind Paris' Pigalle red-light district.

Its bold undulations communicate sensuality (or "sensuousness"
– depending on focus), while the fine *abaca* weave gives it an
airy look and allows the piece to occupy space almost without
the weight.

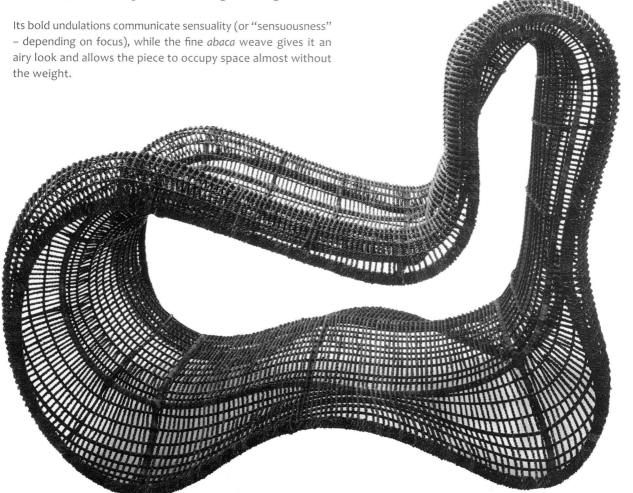

dining table

MATERIALS: alder wood top, stone cast bases with cast aluminum stretcher
SIZE: H 78.7 x W 213.4 x D 119.4 cm
FINISH: verona for the table top (blonde wood tone with light distressing); natural antique for the stonecast posts; dark antique aluminum for the stretcher
DESIGNER: winsor white
MANUFACTURER: maitland-smith
YEAR: 1999

Reminiscent of the Italian Renaissance style, this dining table is an example of furniture combining different materials.

ernest hemingway®
collection
stand-up desk
bar stool

MATERIALS: (stand-up desk) laminated genuine top hide, solid brass hardware, alder wood frame; (bar stool) hand-carved leather back with Hemingway's insignia, the Blue Marlin; woven leather seat, alder wood frame
SIZE: stand-up desk H 123.5 x W 116 x D 66.5 cm; bar stool H 103.6 x W 50 x D 56 cm
DESIGNER: daniel wistehuff, sr.
MANUFACTURER: castilex
CLIENT: exclusive to thomasville furniture
YEAR: 1999

The Ernest Hemingway® Collection was inspired by the prolific writer's life in seclusion which was the time he used writing his manuscripts and novels.

The stand-up desk was inspired by stories that Ernest Hemingway would write standing up due to his back ailment.

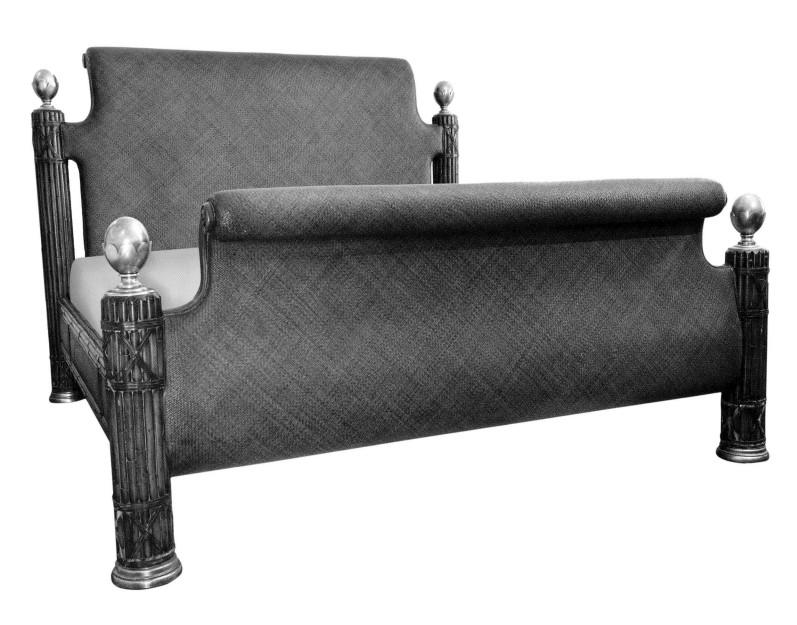

ernest hemingway®
collection
kilimanjaro bed

MATERIALS: rattan, aluminum, wood, twill
SIZE: H 159.4 x W 221 x D 252.7 cm
DESIGNER: daniel wistehuff, sr.
MANUFACTURER: mehitabel furniture inc.
CLIENT: exclusive to thomasville furniture
YEAR: 1999

This signature bed from the Ernest Hemingway® Collection was inspired by the author's "African theme" that lasted many years.

The "ostrich-egg" finial conjures images of North Africa in tribute to Hemingway, the fearless hunter and adventurer.

centerpiece collection

MATERIALS: shells and silver-plated casted solid bronze
SIZE: (left) H 11.7 x W 16.5 x D 9.8 cm;
(right) H 53 x W 20.3 x D 10.5 cm
DESIGNER: arden siarot
MANUFACTURER: arden classic inc.
YEAR: 2000

Seashells and coconut shells were used by English and Continental goldsmiths from the 15th to 16th centuries to escape from the rules of symmetry and balance the design.

The Centerpiece Collection by Arden Classic is elegant with a timeless beauty that can be used as centerpieces.

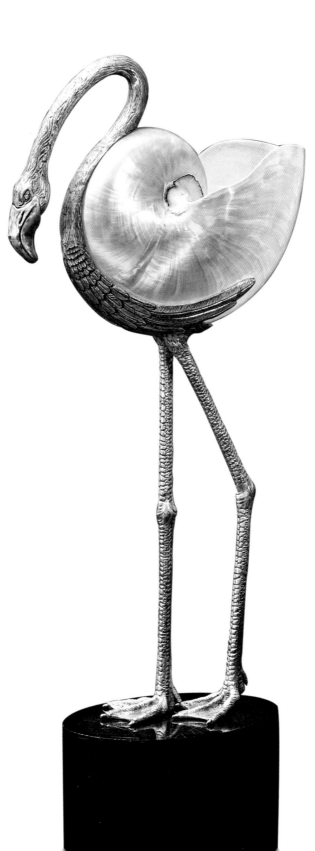

croissant collection
coffee table & end table
easy arm chair

MATERIALS: (indoor) *abaca* rope and *buri*, nylon twine, steel; (outdoor) polyethylene fiber, nylon twine, steel
SIZE: medium coffee table H 35 x Dia. 118.5 cm with table top Dia. 100 cm; end table H 40 x Dia. 68 cm with table top: Dia. 50 cm; easy arm chair H 68 x W 103 x D 95 cm
DESIGNER: kenneth cobonpue
MANUFACTURER: interior crafts of the islands inc.
YEAR: 2000

That typically French pastry – the croissant – lends its delicate crescent shape and distinct central crest to furniture crafted for indulgence.

As ergonomic as it is visually relaxing, the chair has gentle slopes that glide down to the armrests as if to encourage a posture of leisure. *Abaca* rope tied over a hand-sculpted frame provides a feast for the senses with its stimulating texture and invigorating natural hues.

Abaca rope in different diameters is woven expertly into various designs of chairs, arm chairs and loveseats. Thin ropes are also laminated on wooden carcasses or other surfaces to enhance the look of tables, cabinets and dressers.

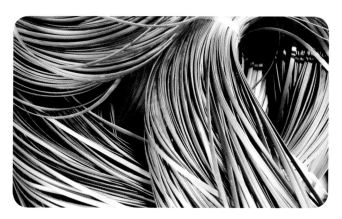

DEDON Fiber – made of HDPE (High Density Polyethylene), highly resistant to cold and heat, UV-resistant, environment friendly (100% recyclable, toxin-free), possessing high tensile strength, and able to withstand exposure to sun, snow and saltwater

daydream

MATERIAL: aluminum frame wrapped in DEDON Fiber
SIZE: H 214 x W 215 x D 139 cm
DESIGNER: richard frinier
MANUFACTURER: DEDON
YEAR: 2000

Inspired by the traditional craft of weaving, which brought DEDON to Cebu in the first place. From the seemingly ordinary craft of basketry, the DAYDREAM Collection was developed using the traditional weaving referred to as "caning".

The collection channels exotic Morocco and dreamy "Arabian Nights" images of magic carpet rides.

It is the embodiment of true outdoor furniture – an invitation to relax and give one's imagination free rein. A back panel and side panels could be added. Sheer panels can also be hung from poles to create a canopy, providing more privacy than just an umbrella.

gantang
corner chair
side chair

MATERIALS: wood frame with gold leaf accent
SIZE: corner chair H 66 x W 68.9 x D 68.9 cm;
side chair H 94 x W 43.2 x D 58.4 cm
DESIGNER: corito escario yu
STYLISTIC VARIATIONS: arm chair
MANUFACTURER: apy cane incorporated
YEAR: 2000

Gantang is a Cebuano word for a cup or square pail that is used as unit of measurement for rice. The designer's friend named the piece, reminded of a *gantang* by the square shape and accent.

greigo
greigo ii side chair
bed & night stand

MATERIALS: wood frame with twisted *abaca* inlay or gold leaf accent (side chairs); wood frame with *abaca* inlay (night table and bed)
DESIGNER: corito escario yu
STYLISTIC VARIATIONS: greigo bench, greigo i side chair and arm chair, greigo ii arm chair
MANUFACTURER: apy cane incorporated
CLIENT: noreen yu/julie yu
YEAR: 2000

The piece was designed to use *abaca*, a local material in a modern context, and to use an ancient Greek pattern for accents. The goal was to use simple forms that were easy to mix in modern or eclectic homes. With the idea of "minimalism", the designer visualized an uncluttered room with very few pieces and the furniture being the focal point.

cutgrass vase

MATERIALS: sig-id vine, fiber glass, resin
SIZE: H 48 to 71.5 x Dia. 7 to 9.5 cm
DESIGNER: luisa robinson
MANUFACTURER: detalia aurora inc.
YEAR: 2000

The designer was inspired by long blades of grass
moving in the wind.

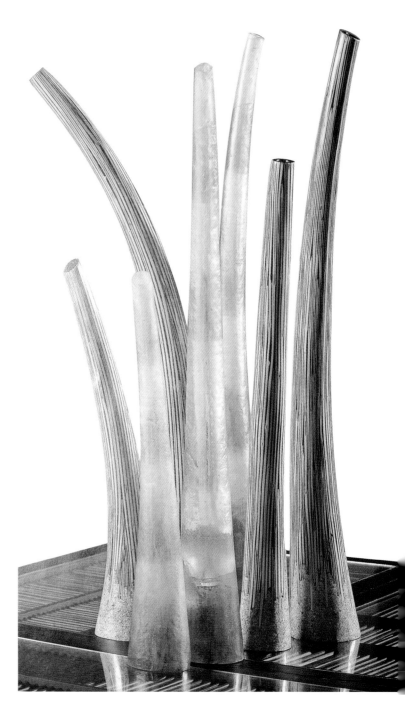

orbit

MATERIAL: aluminum frame with DEDON Fiber
SIZE: H 193 x Dia. 165 cm
DESIGNER: richard frinier
MANUFACTURER: DEDON
YEAR: 2001

Orbit sprang from the desire to create a small, enclosed universe – an island in space.

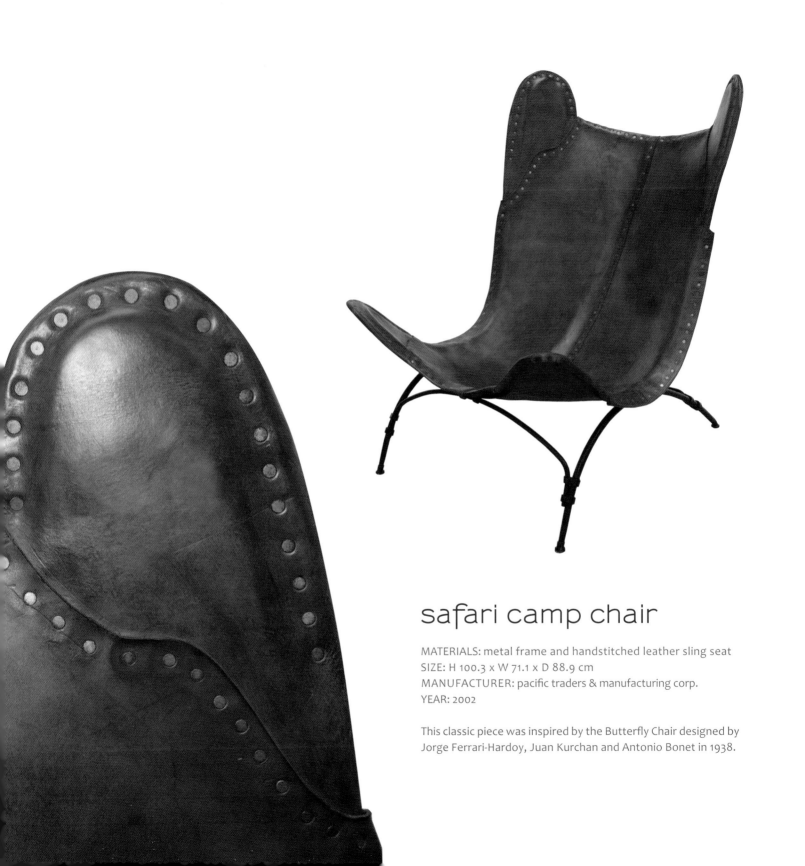

safari camp chair

MATERIALS: metal frame and handstitched leather sling seat
SIZE: H 100.3 x W 71.1 x D 88.9 cm
MANUFACTURER: pacific traders & manufacturing corp.
YEAR: 2002

This classic piece was inspired by the Butterfly Chair designed by
Jorge Ferrari-Hardoy, Juan Kurchan and Antonio Bonet in 1938.

camp chair

MATERIALS: beech wood frame and handstitched
leather sling seat
SIZE: H 117.5 x W 66.7 x D 78.1 cm
MANUFACTURER: castilex
YEAR: 2002

Similar to the Safari Camp Chair on page 142, the Camp Chair is
an updated version of the Butterfly Chair's sling seat.

console table

MATERIAL: mahogany plate #13 veneer and *lauan* solids
SIZE: H 63.5 x W 66 x D 50.8 cm
DESIGNER: gregg huettel
MANUFACTURER: pacific traders & manufacturing corp.
CLIENT: ethan allen
YEAR: 2003

The designer's intention was to make an artistic conversation piece that could function both as a tea table and as a free-standing console table that could be placed anywhere in the home. This item utilized Cebu's talents of veneering, piercing curved panels and carving wood. The design itself blends English furniture disciplines with a loose flair of decorative West Indies-inspired scroll work that allows it to be used in both formal and semi-formal settings.

armoire

MATERIALS: solid alder wood with woven caning and cast
brass accents
SIZE: H 233.7 x W 151.1 x D 59.7 cm
DESIGNER: winsor white
MANUFACTURER: maitland-smith
YEAR: 2003

Inspired by the simplicity in design and décor of the French
Provincial style, the interior of this armoire has been designed
to be used as a television cabinet as well.

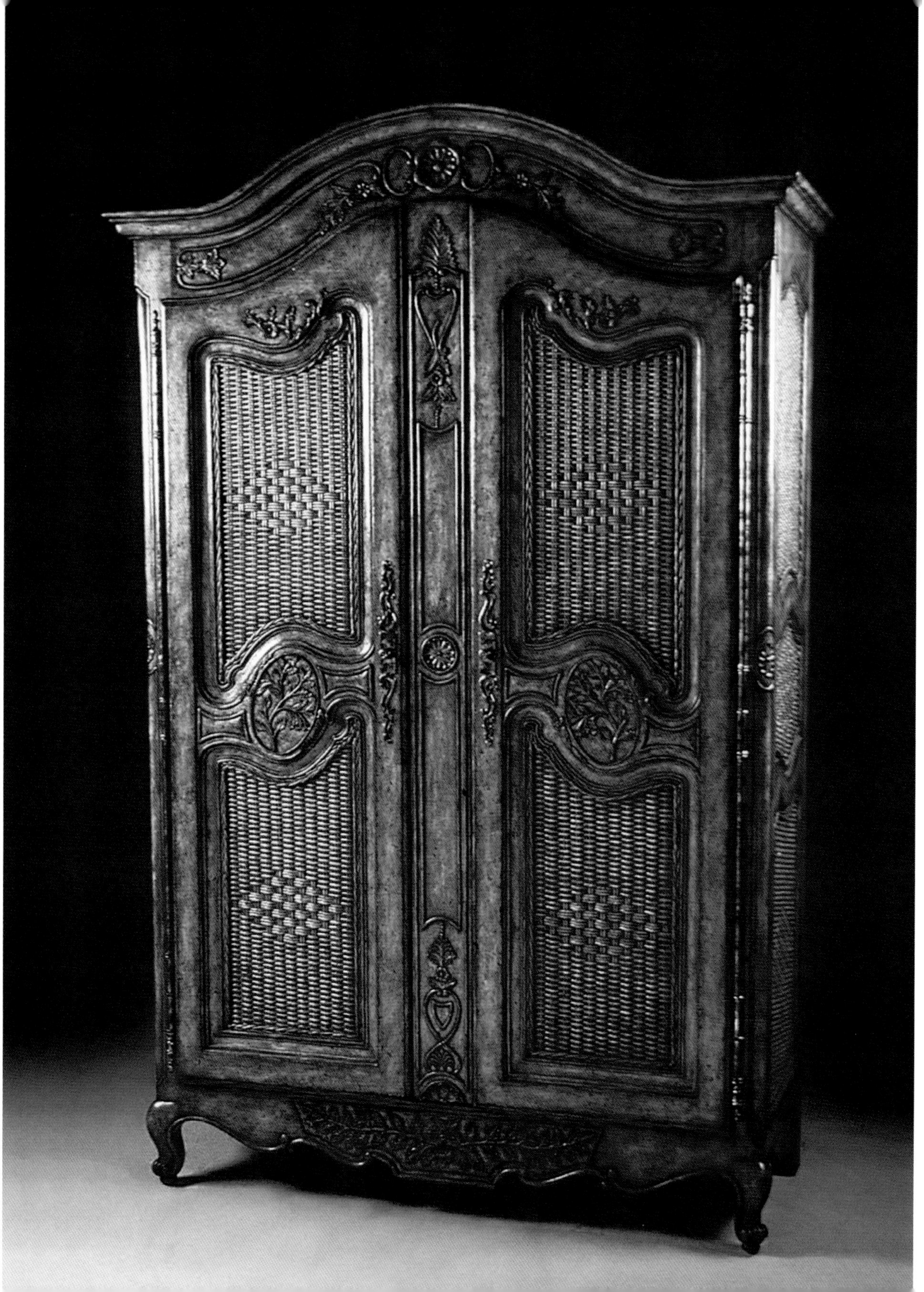

148

bandana occasional chair

MATERIALS: wicker with metal chrome base
SIZE: H 86.4 x W 81.3 x D 65.4 cm
DESIGNER: bernice montenegro
MANUFACTURER: pacific traders & manufacturing corp.
YEAR: 2003

Inspired by the designer's then eight-year-old daughter who loved wearing bandanas, the Bandana Occasional Chair gives the impression of ease, comfort and youth.

kai 'arc' floor lamp

MATERIALS: *buri*, wire, *abaca*, handmade paper
SIZE: large floor lamp H 250 x W 274.5 x D 84 cm
DESIGNER: kenneth cobonpue
STYLISTIC VARIATION: kai tripod floor lamp
MANUFACTURER: hive
YEAR: 2003

Sustainable, traditional materials quickly bring to mind the earthy allure of Oriental-style lighting.

Traditional materials create warmth and recall the romance of the East.

totong coffee table

MATERIALS: bamboo with veneer top
SIZE: H 50.8 x Dia. 101.6 cm
DESIGNER: fernando "astik" villarin
MANUFACTURER: pacific traders & manufacturing corp.
YEAR: 2003

The designer was inspired by his childhood memories of his late father's manner of slicing their favorite "*kamansi*" and the unique look of the jackfruit-like vegetable once sliced. The Totong Coffee Table is a delightful and organic design.

tilt collection
sofa
arm chair

MATERIAL: *lauan* or walnut
SIZE: sofa H 62 x W 210 x D 93 cm;
arm chair H 62 x W 92 x D 96 cm
DESIGNER: kenneth cobonpue
STYLISTIC VARIATIONS: loveseat
MANUFACTURER: interior crafts of the islands inc.
YEAR: 2003

The Tilt Collection, inspired by the architectural concept of the 'tilt', embraces the reality of recline as a pose of ease. This collection inclines to a very comfortable and stylish direction.

The linear and dynamic qualities of its signature slant embody masculinity.

153

daybed

MATERIALS: mahogany, rattan, wicker
SIZE: H 61 x W 204.2 x D 91.4 cm
DESIGNER: rey g. ipong
MANUFACTURER: casa cebuana
YEAR: 2004

This lounge-type bench was inspired by a kettle with its soft,
rounded shape that exudes coziness and style.

voyage collection
bed

MATERIALS: *abaca* or *buri*, nylon twine, steel
SIZE: H 160 x W 168 to 205 x D 253 to 260 cm
DESIGNER: kenneth cobonpue
MANUFACTURER: interior crafts of the islands inc.
YEAR: 2004

The sleek form of sailboats and the typical curved shapes of reed boats bring to mind adventurers' voyages through the ages, and a similar journey taken by the dreamer in his sleep.

gold fish with stone base

MATERIALS: bamboo, rattan and stonecast
DESIGNER: marguerite lhuillier
MANUFACTURER: infini
YEAR: 2005

halo lamp

MATERIALS: nylon strings, metal frame
SIZE: H 146 x Dia. 70 cm
DESIGNER: kenneth cobonpue
MANUFACTURER: hive
YEAR: 2005

Two iconic Christian symbols served as inspiration for this lamp: the halo and the fisherman's net. By combining these two symbols, the Halo Lamp becomes a beautiful expression of light.

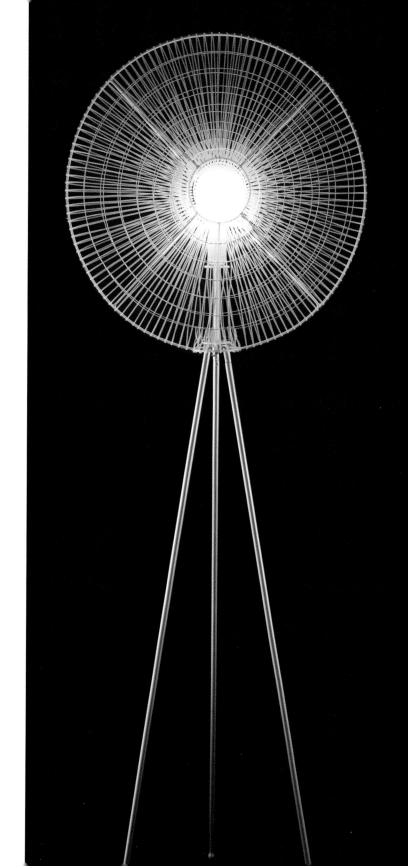

arm chair

MATERIALS: mahogany solids woven with carahide leather
SIZE: H 107.3 x W 64.1 x D 66.4 cm
DESIGNER: winsor white
MANUFACTURER: mehitabel furniture inc.
CLIENTS: robb & stucky, nuebo tienda
YEAR: 2005

Its richness in color, texture, and detail appeals to the sophisticated tastes of the high-end U.S. market.

coffee table

MATERIALS: mahogany solids, laminated mactan
stone top with coconut inlay
SIZE: H 50.8 x W 119.4 x D 119.4 cm
DESIGNER: winsor white
MANUFACTURER: mehitabel furniture inc.
CLIENTS: robb & stucky, nuebo tienda
YEAR: 2005

This piece has the smooth, clean, geometric look of modern
furniture. Every line exudes a clear cosmopolitan vibe.

web collection
lounge chair
two-seater chair

MATERIALS: metal and epoxy-based resins
SIZE: lounge chair H 73 x W 80 x D 68 cm;
two-seater chair H 70 x W 160 x W 160 cm
DESIGNER: ramir bonghanoy
STYLISTIC VARIATIONS: coffee table base, mirror frame,
lounge chair, two-seater chair
MANUFACTURER: bon-ace fashion tools, inc.
YEAR: 2005

The Web Collection was inspired by the delicate, lacy beauty of
the neural web and sea corals. The lounge chair is embellished
with shell to simulate Poseidon's coral throne.

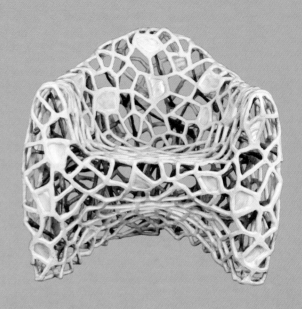

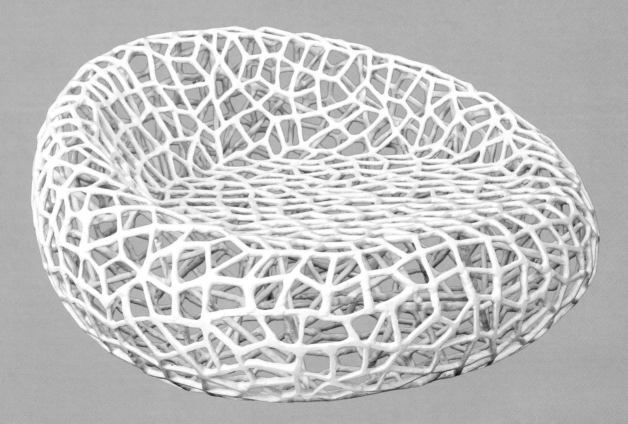

end table

MATERIAL: nickel plated brass ferrules; gmelina solids, cherry crown, quarters and prima vera quarters veneer
SIZE: H 73.7 x Dia. 81.3 cm
DESIGNER: gregg huettel
MANUFACTURER: wicker & vine, inc.
CLIENT: chelsea house
YEAR: 2006

This table blends transitional legs with Art Deco scalloped aprons that are topped off with a beautiful cherry sunburst top. The designer, Gregg Huettel, wanted to achieve a strong finish contrast between the silver leaf 'Deco' style and the warm brown cherry finish. The nickel ferrules add the additional pop.

mandalay
console table

MATERIALS: rattan and rattan caning
SIZE: H 90.2 x W 137.2 x D 45.7 cm
DESIGNER: rene ybañez
MANUFACTURER: obra cebuana inc.
YEAR: 2006

The Mandalay Console Table was inspired by Oriental and
Spanish antique furniture. The rattan and caning used create
a very natural feeling for this collection.

planter
(banana leaf collection)

MATERIALS: rattan frame with *abaca*, seagrass
and *lampakanay* weaving
SIZE: H 142.2 x Dia. 48.3 cm
DESIGNER: fernando "astik" villarin
MANUFACTURER: pacific traders & manufacturing corp.
YEAR: 2006

Inspired by the different textures and undulations on a banana
leaf, these planter baskets are simple both in lines and detail.

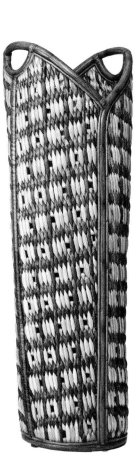

Lampakanay or *Cat-tail* is a greenish to beige fiber that is usually manufactured into ropes, braids or just a twisted twine. Lampakanay comes in different diameters and lengths. The entire or split stems of lampakanay are used for making coarse bags, baskets, and rope for furniture trimmings.

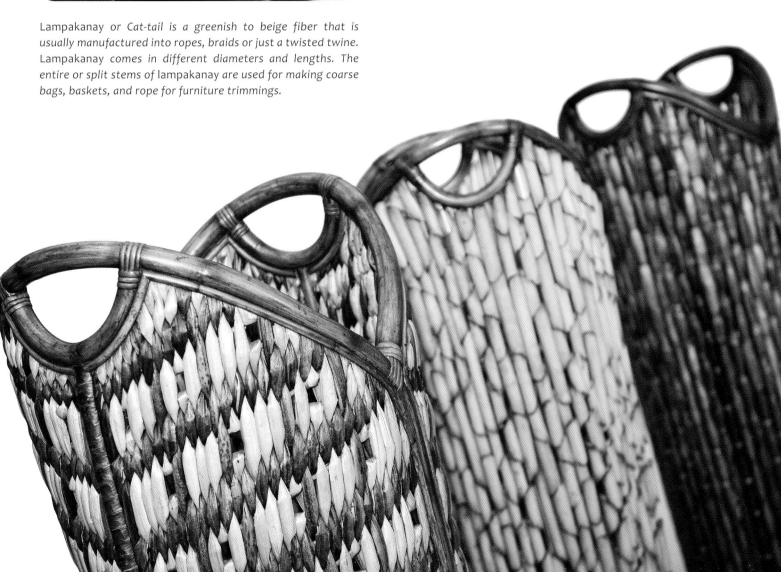

othello
two-seater sofa

MATERIALS: rattan frame, *arurog* deco, z-matting
SIZE: H 85.7 x W 145.4 x D 87.3 cm
DESIGNER: carlo s. tanseco
MANUFACTURER: castilex
entry to cebu x 2007
YEAR: 2006-2007

Arurog is the thin-jointed stem of a rattan pole used especially for furniture weaving and decor.

¹ancient chinese raincoat with stand

MATERIALS: rattan, *abaca* and wood
DESIGNER: marguerite lhuillier
MANUFACTURER: infini
YEAR: 2007

²bamboo polymer deco

MATERIALS: polymer and rattan
DESIGNER: marguerite lhuillier
MANUFACTURER: infini
YEAR: 2007

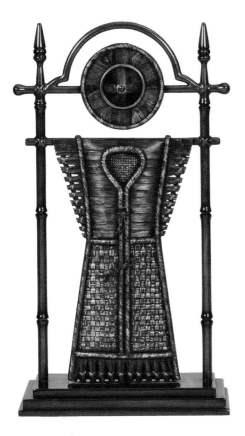

1

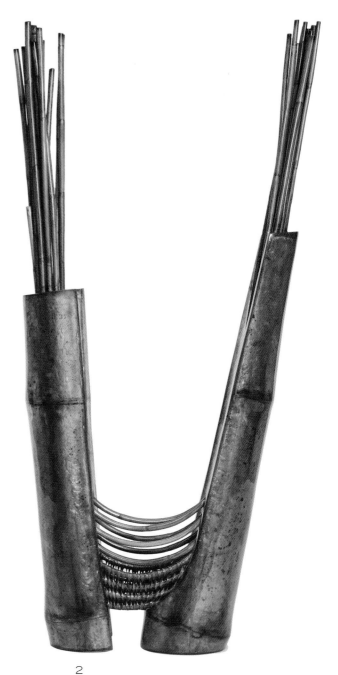

2

ovium collection
mirror

MATERIALS: oval shaped shell inlays and
hammered stainless steel
SIZE: H 128 x W 128 x D 11 cm
DESIGNER: ramir bonghanoy
STYLISTIC VARIATIONS: vase, planters, accent furniture
MANUFACTURER: bon-ace fashion tools, inc.
YEAR: 2007

This mirror frame from the Ovium Collection of Bon-Ace resembles a pile of leaves that invites anyone who sees it to "go and touch", leaving a circular imprint at the center.

The other pieces from this collection show that fluidity in look can be achieved by manipulation or arrangement of materials.

baud bench

MATERIALS: *arurog* with metal frame
SIZE: H 58.7 x Dia. 129 cm
DESIGNER: vito selma
STYLISTIC VARIATION: cocktail table
MANUFACTURER: stonesets international inc.
CLIENTS: globe west, varya home design, ito kish
YEAR: 2007

Few languages capture the essence of the wave quite like the
Cebuano dialect, in both its fluidity and its solidness, curling
inwards and out of itself.

The intricate work and craftsmanship involved in the design,
and the combination of materials, make this bench not just a
seat but a sculptural masterpiece as well.

The Baud Bench is part of a collection that pays tribute to the
ocean that has forever kept the island city of Cebu home in its
undulating embrace.

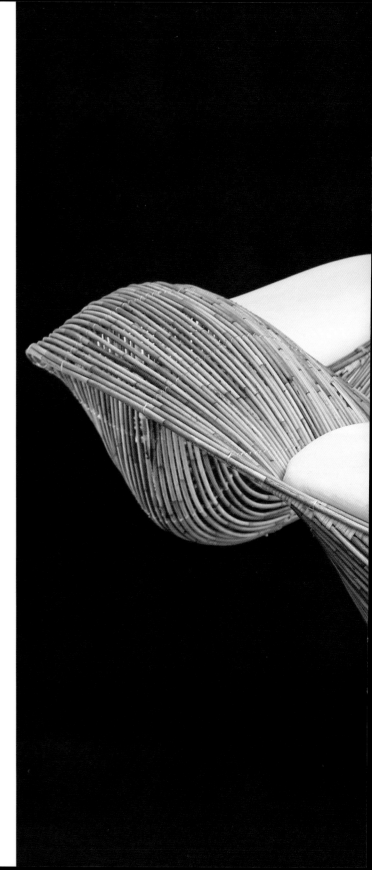

canasta
sofa
circular sofa

MATERIAL: polyethylene fiber, aluminum frame, satined
stainless steel base
SIZE: sofa H 121.9 x W 226.1 x D 108 cm;
circular sofa H 87.9 x W 181.3 x D 185.1 cm
DESIGNER: patricia urquiola
STYLISTIC VARIATIONS: high and low backrest linear sofas
and arm chairs, sunbed
MANUFACTURER: pacific traders & manufacturing corp.
CLIENT: b&b italia
YEAR: 2007

Patricia Urquiola approached the outdoors starting from
the theme woven patterns – reviving and personalizing the
concept with a traditional look in mind, but giving it a decisively
contemporary look without using too much nostalgic influence.
The seating elements in this collection were inspired by the
conical shape and weave that is similar to baskets. Traditional
Vienna straw, with its decorative geometric shape, is also a
model for these pieces. The traditional pattern was amplified,
increasing it to macro-proportions and was used to make a
dramatic line of comfortable chairs and sofas.

Ideal for the swimming pool area or the garden lawn, these
chairs are like pieces of "land art" that harmonize with the
surrounding scenery.

Capiz Shells are marine bivalve commonly found in Philippine coastal waters, such as Bataan and Cavite, and are characterized by a large thin flat translucent shell. The shells are cleaned and graded before being used as a decorative element in some Filipino houses, furniture and home accessories.

176

console cabinet with matching mirror frame

MATERIALS: black pen shell, brown pen shell, *cabebe* shell
DESIGNER: ronnie fernando go
MANUFACTURER: jcl export inc.
YEAR: 2007

This console cabinet with matching mirror frame were inspired by the beautiful and exotic spiral shape of high quality seashells. The style is modern but still retains a classic and elegant look.

longhorn
occasional chair
ottoman

MATERIAL: faux animal horn and bonded leather in
ivory finish (seats) and rawhide (back)
SIZE: occasional chair H 81 x W 77 x D 75 cm
DESIGNER: luisa robinson
MANUFACTURER: detalia aurora inc.
YEAR: 2007

This set was inspired by the symmetry and flowing
lines of animal horns.

slatted walnut chair

MATERIAL: solid walnut
SIZE: H 87.6 x W 52.1 x D 58.4 cm
MANUFACTURER: pacific traders & manufacturing corp.
CLIENT: exclusive to the mcguire furniture company
YEAR: 2007

A part of the McGuire Designs Collection, the precise nature of the slatted style of this chair demands a high level of craftsmanship. The slats and joints are of mortise-and-tenon construction, and the components have been carefully selected and placed so that the wood grain is positioned to maximize compression and tensile strength.

A rich satin finish reveals the character and beauty of the wood. A testament to the fact that sometimes the simplest of forms can be the most difficult to execute, this chair is poised, with fluid lines and impeccable construction that by no means sacrifice comfort.

tray table

MATERIAL: brass, z-mat inlay, philippine mahogany solids
SIZE: H 63.5 x W 72.4 x D 38.1 cm
DESIGNER: gregg huettel
MANUFACTURER: pacific traders & manufacturing corp.
YEAR: 2007

This fun tray table is inspired by a gentleman's umbrella that has been transformed into an 'X' base that supports two trays. It is a flashy conversation piece that also provides a serving function with its removable top tray. It is small enough to be positioned anywhere your entertaining needs are required. The nickel plated brass accents really make this item shine.

Z-mat is made from rattan skin that was woven using a machine.

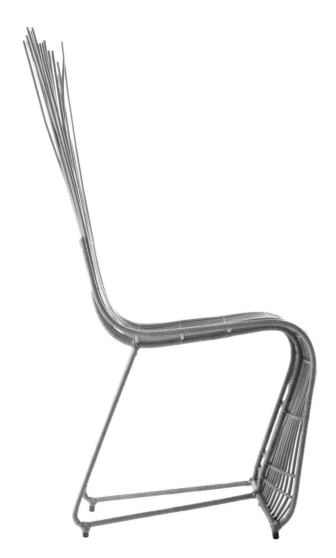

yoda

MATERIALS: (indoor) rattan, nylon twine, steel;
(outdoor) pvc, nylon twine, steel
SIZE: H 134 x W 63 x D 70 cm
DESIGNER: kenneth cobonpue
STYLISTIC VARIATIONS: easy chair, side chair, bar stool,
sectional sofa, ottoman, coffee and end tables
MANUFACTURER: interior crafts of the islands inc.
YEAR: 2007

The character "Yoda" from the "Star Wars" film series
personifies that deep sense of inner balance we all strive for.
Such a delicate balance may also be seen in the juxtaposition
of simplistic form and striking detail in the blades of grass on
a savannah.

Using natural material tension, the collection features rattan's
aesthetic and functional versatility. The novel backrest gives
Yoda its unique character, a display that offers comfort
disguised in randomness reminiscent of nature's surprises.

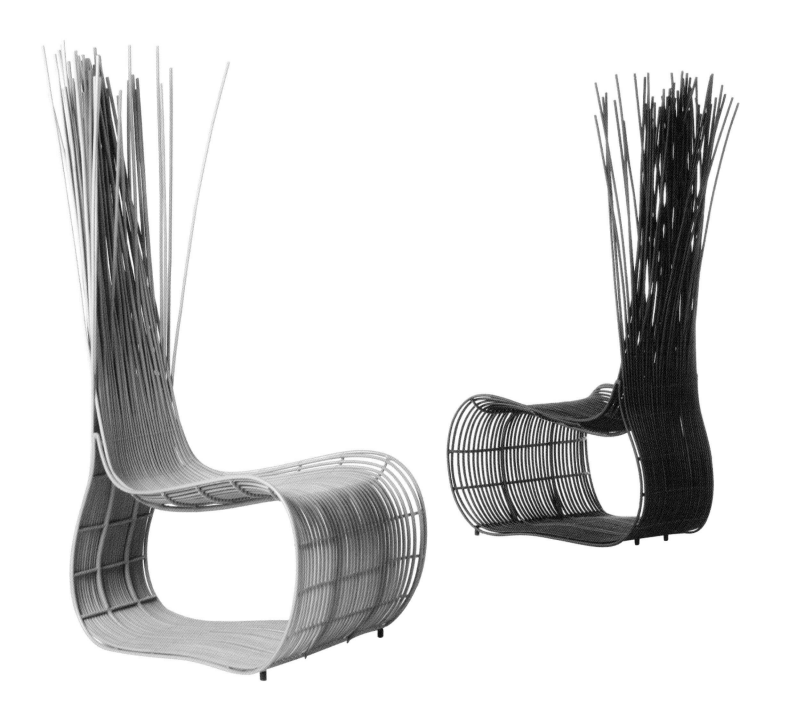

console table

MATERIAL: rosewood crown, quarter satinwood, cherry
gummy quarter veneer, philippine mahogany solids
SIZE: H 86.4 x W 165.1 x D 53.3 cm
DESIGNER: gregg huettel
MANUFACTURER: pacific traders & manufacturing corp.
CLIENT: bernard christianson
YEAR: 2008

Gregg Huettel designed this large-scale console to be used for
entry foyers and dining areas. It is made with rosewood, which
Huettel considers one of the world's most beautiful woods.
Even though the rosewood is stunning by itself, he added
lighter satin wood veneers and brass hardwood as contrasts.
The hand-rubbed high sheen finish creates a jewel of an item
with amazing depth and clarity.

gemstone fish

MATERIALS: wrought iron and philippine gemstones
(green jasper, red jasper, scenic agate)
SIZE: H 17.1 to 23.5 x W 13.3 to 19.1 x D 3.8 to 7.6 cm
DESIGNER: janice minor
MANUFACTURER: janice minor
YEAR: 2008

Inspired by a school of angelfish, these gemstone fish by
Janice Minor can be welded together in large numbers
as wall art.

*Agate is a microcrystalline variety of silica characterized
by its fineness of grain and brightness of color. Agates are
usually associated with volcanic rocks and can be common
in certain metamorphic rocks.*

*Agates are usually used in arts and crafts to make
ornaments but can also be used to make mortars and
pestles. They have been used for centuries as leather
burnishing tools.*

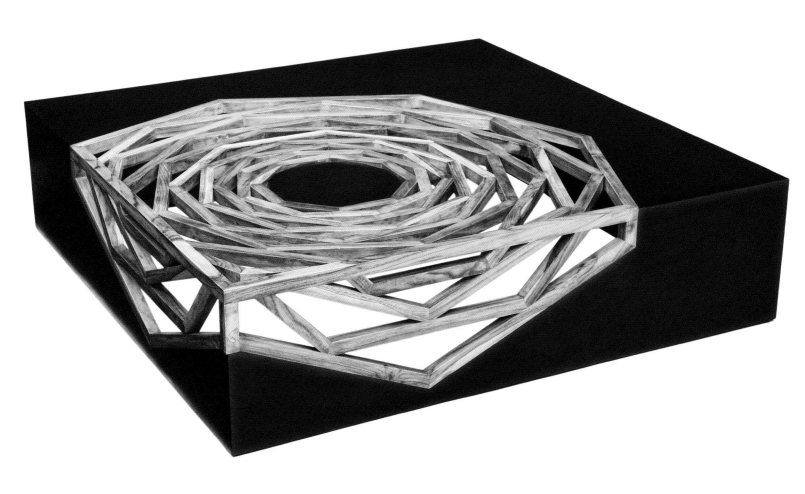

hanako cocktail table

MATERIALS: teak wood and veneer on plywood
SIZE: H 30.5 x W 120 x D 120 cm
DESIGNER: vito selma
STYLISTIC VARIATION: console table
MANUFACTURER: stonesets international inc.
CLIENTS: red brown, varya home designs, ito kish
YEAR: 2008

This table was created to respond to the desire to embrace nature by inviting it into our homes.

The pieces in this collection creates contrast between the shiny or glossy finish and the naked wood in its natural color. Geometric floral patterns on the wood add softness to the design.

lasang
side chair

MATERIAL: rattan
SIZE: H 101.6 x W 52 x D 67.3 cm
DESIGNER: fernando "astik" villarin
STYLISTIC VARIATIONS: arm chair, side table
MANUFACTURER: pacific traders & manufacturing corp.
YEAR: 2008

The designer was inspired by his memories of a lifetime full of challenges, when a day is started by collecting firewood in the forest as a means of livelihood. Intentionally matchless furniture, the Lasang Collection gives the impression of the wild ambience of the forest, replete with vines wrapped around trees and images of Tarzan in the wild.

lux suspension lamp

MATERIALS: acrylic (plastic housing) and dried fish scales
SIZE: 20 or 30 cm square
DESIGNER: joseph laxina
MANUFACTURER: hive
YEAR: 2008

The Lux Suspension Lamp is an intriguing display of illuminated fish scales appearing as natural, petal-like growths framed within a cube.

maze coffee table

MATERIALS: rattan core and copper wire
SIZE: base H 29.6 x W 91 X D 91 cm
DESIGNER: debbie palao
STYLISTIC VARIATIONS: end table, dining table, coffee table
MANUFACTURER: design ventures cebu, inc.
YEAR: 2008

Passing by a construction site one day, the designer found the scaffoldings intriguing against the receding sun – by turns fragile yet sturdy, randomly placed yet deliberately structural.

The natural elements contrasted by the industrial sheen of the copper grounds what seems like a confusion of vertical and horizontal lines.

The designer shared that one contract project actually used this piece as a sculpture.

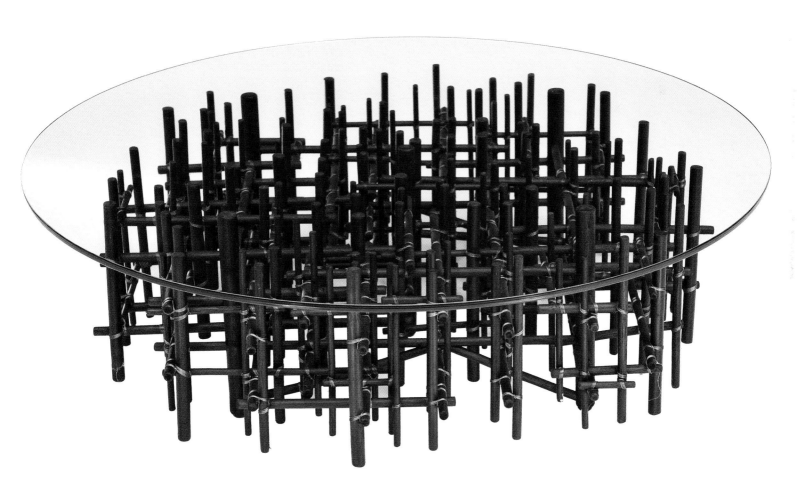

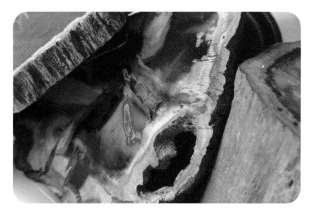

Petrified wood is the result of a tree having turned completely into stone by the process of permineralization. All the organic materials have been replaced with minerals, such as quartz, while retaining the original structure of the wood.

petrified wood
console table

MATERIAL: petrified wood and resin
SIZE: H 82.55 x W 139.7 x D 43.2 cm
FINISH: polished and buffed wood
DESIGNER: janice minor
MANUFACTURER: janice minor
CLIENT: oggetti, batuka
YEAR: 2008

For this piece, the designer was inspired by the natural look of petrified wood boulders cut in half.

ravel

MATERIAL: polyethylene fiber, aluminum and steel frames
SIZE: H 78.1 x W 158.4 x D 98.4 cm
DESIGNER: patricia urquiola
MANUFACTURER: pacific traders & manufacturing corp.
CLIENT: b&b italia
YEAR: 2008

Drawing inspiration from field experimentation in the Philippines, the Ravel Collection is a further detailed study of the woven theme. The modular element of this collection allows the pieces to form linear or corner seats or chaise lounge end units. Pouf elements can be used both as intervals between seats and to increase seat depth.

salbaro bench table

MATERIALS: coco twigs, rattan fiber, metal, plywood
SIZE: H 40.6 x W 248.9 x D 94 cm
FINISH: coco round core in white resin
DESIGNER: clayton tugonon
MANUFACTURER: classical geometry
CLIENTS: gorsia design pvt ltd, weylandts, habitat
YEAR: 2008

The designer had the brilliant idea of making this table when he was eating a piece of salbaro bread. This piece can also be used as a bench.

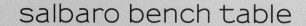

swirl side table

MATERIALS: chrome-plated metal base and walnut veneer top
SIZE: H 55.9 x Dia. 61 cm
DESIGNER: bernice montenegro
MANUFACTURER: pacific traders & manufacturing corp.
YEAR: 2008

Inspired by the desire for an eye-catching modern piece different from typical designs, the Swirl Side Table's chrome base is reminiscent of a hurricane funnel, communicating transparency and continuous movement.

tuskany
dining table
console

MATERIALS: faux horns, chrome-plated steel or stainless
steel, glass or hand in-laid natural turnsole
SIZE: dining table H 73.8 x W 64.5 x D 55.9 cm with table top
Dia. 130 cm; console H 77 x W 88 x D 35 cm with table top
W 152 x D 46 cm
DESIGNER: luisa robinson
MANUFACTURER: detalia aurora inc.
YEAR: 2008

The different beautiful forms of animal horns such as longhorn and elephant tusks inspired these pieces. The collection
actually started with one leather chair with arms and front
legs made of two sweeping and continuous faux longhorns
(Longhorn Occasional Chair).

The Tuskany tables relive the excitement of the safari with
faux horns intricately hand-finished to resemble real tusks.

star storage

MATERIAL: resin
SIZE: H 43.2 x W 43.2 x D 43.2 cm
COLORS: black with black sand inlay, white with black inlay
DESIGNER: joseph crisanto
IMPRESSION: stacking storage boxes
MANUFACTURER: apy cane incorporated
YEAR: 2008

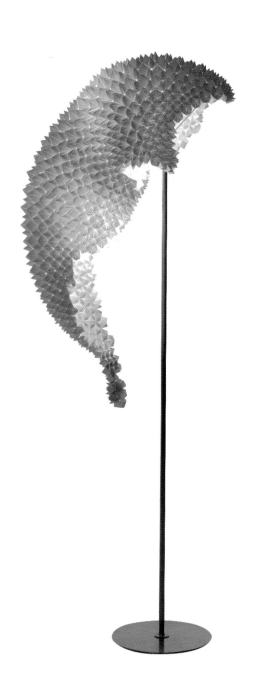

dragon's tail lamps
floor lamp
hanging lamp

MATERIALS: paper, stainless steel, fiberglass resin
SIZE: hanging lamp H 44 to 107 x W 29 to 36 x D 23 cm
DESIGNER: luisa robinson
MANUFACTURER: hive
YEAR: 2008-2009

Nostalgia for childhood and memories of bedtime stories about knights, princesses and dragons brought about the creation of these uniquely shaped lamps.

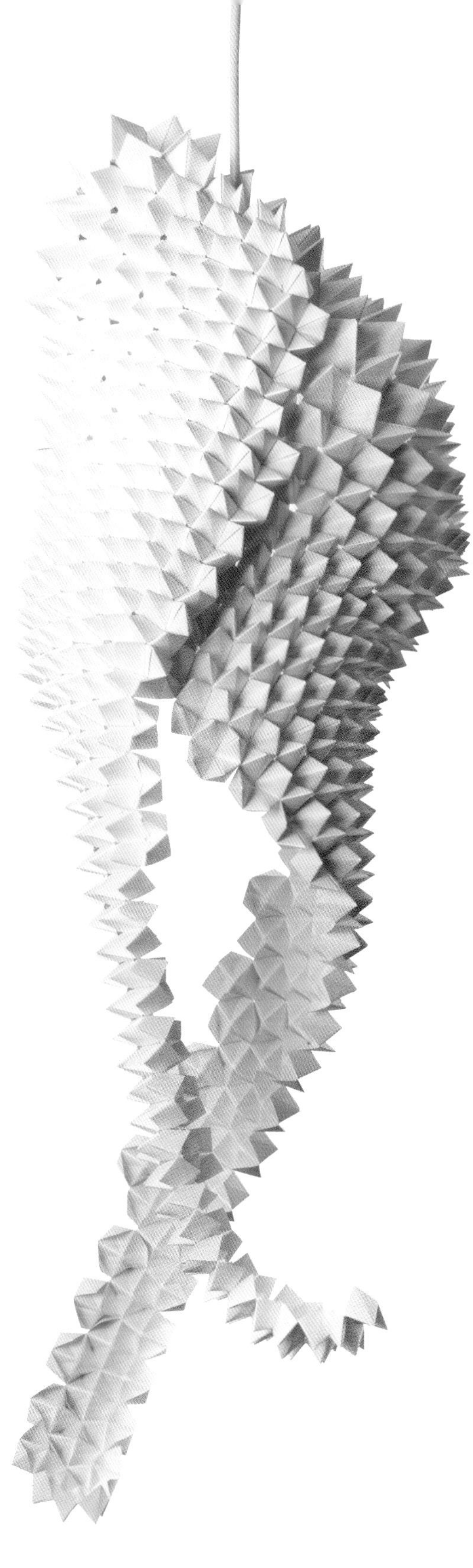

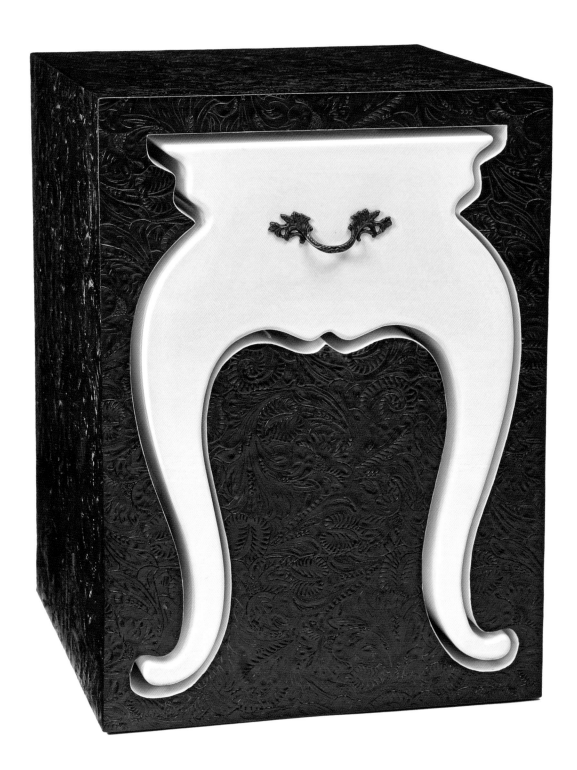

212

amadeus
occasional table
(set of 2) ambulante style

MATERIAL: laminated wood, bonded leather in engraved and embossed floral pattern
SIZE: H 60 x W 45 x D 45 cm
DESIGNER: paula rodriguez
MANUFACTURER: detalia aurora inc.
YEAR: 2009

This set is a merging of past styles from the Baroque period with modern trends; the contour and elegance of curves are married to practicality and sleek lines. The baroque shapes juxtaposed with a modern silhouette deliver a witty take on the classic rococo style.

Two tables in one space-saving footprint; one table is an insert fitted with a brass handle and hidden space-runner to ensure smooth pull-out and push-in. These make up a playful and fun contemporary piece designed to represent a union of inspiration that translates into current fashion.

chest

MATERIAL: shagreen leather, philippine mahogany solids and daniela quarters
SIZE: H 94.9 x W 88.9 x D 49.2 cm
DESIGNER: gregg huettel
MANUFACTURER: pacific traders & manufacturing corp.
YEAR: 2009

Shagreen was used extensively during the Art Deco period. The designer took the opportunity to use an environmentally friendly 'faux' shagreen to flow between the curved framework of an elegant chest form. While the overall form is simple, the effect is strong. A clean and simple design actually demands more precision with joinery, inlay work and finishing than traditional styles. The designer had wanted the nickel-plated hardware to be simple yet as functional as possible.

chest

MATERIAL: alder, cherry quarters, walnut quarters with black lines, prima vera quarters, maple quarters, rosewood and mahogany solids
SIZE: H 95.3 x W 119.4 x 50.8 cm
DESIGNER: gregg huettel
MANUFACTURER: pacific traders & manufacturing corp.
CLIENT: bernard christianson
YEAR: 2009

The Italians are indeed furniture masters and have always been very talented with veneer marquetry and decorative ornament. This bow front chest proves that Cebuano artisans possess this same veneering talent and can achieve great things when challenged. Almost every part of this chest is covered in veneer, and the detailed reproduction finish really makes this item look like an authentic Italian antique.

bloom lounge chair

MATERIALS: microfiber, resin, steel
SIZE: H 87 x W 105 x D 98 cm
DESIGNER: kenneth cobonpue
STYLISTIC VARIATIONS: easy arm chair, club chair
MANUFACTURER: interior crafts of the islands inc.
YEAR: 2009

The Bloom Collection was inspired by the soft petals of a flower as a thing of strength and beauty.

The meticulous needlework and discrete engineering produce subtly undulating tones and texture.

meryll

MATERIALS: fine *abaca* rope and metal
SIZE: H 93 x W 67 x D 41 cm
FINISH: *abaca* rope is dyed using the ikat dyeing technique
DESIGNER: debbie palao
STYLISTIC VARIATIONS: lounge chairs, bar stool
MANUFACTURER: design ventures cebu, inc.
YEAR: 2009

Inspired by a black bubble skirt the designer's niece wore to work one day, the Meryll chair uses the usual weaving techniques to mimic a crocheted piece and draped loose as in couture. It was named after Meryll Streep having also been inspired by the actress' performance in "The Devil Wears Prada".

poppy lamps
hanging lamp
floor lamp

MATERIALS: handmade paper and laminated mylar
SIZE: Dia. 60 to 100 cm
DESIGNER: christy manguerra
MANUFACTURER: hive
YEAR: 2009

The Poppy Lamps were designed with the intention of bringing the delicate beauty of flowers indoors. The softly glowing petals radiate warmth and femininity.

223

snowman
hanging lamp

MATERIALS: resin tiles and fiber glass
DESIGNER: tony gonzales
MANUFACTURER: raphael legacy inc.
YEAR: 2009

Although presently based in Manila, the designer, Tony Gonzales, was schooled in Cebu. This affinity with Cebu makes him quite attuned to the materials and skills of Cebu's furniture and home accessories community.

He has always pushed the envelope in product design by refusing to be tied down to a single design direction. In this lamp design, a series of orbs appear to be held together by fine slivers of resin.

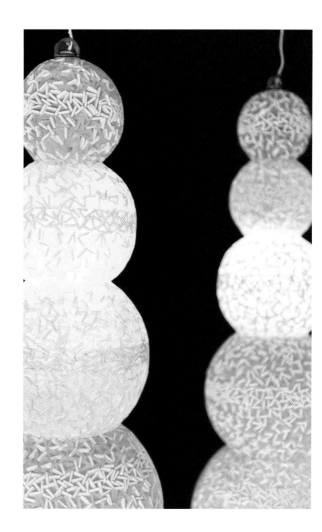

sugbu

MATERIAL: laminated wood cuts
SIZE: H 45.7 x W 330.2 x D 78.7 cm
DESIGNER: fernando "astik" villarin
MANUFACTURER: pacific traders & manufacturing corp.
YEAR: 2009

The Sugbu table is an eco-friendly piece that uses wood cuts found in the furniture factory. It was inspired by Cebu's shape and topography, and Cebuanos' love of nature and country.

curate home collection

MATERIALS: gmelina solids frame with
zambales split weaving
SIZE: H 91.4 x W 60.1 x D 66 cm
DESIGNER: john black
STYLISTIC VARIATIONS: arm chair and side chair
MANUFACTURER: pacific traders & manufacturing corporation
CLIENT: artistica
YEAR: 2009

arm chair

MATERIAL: rattan poles
SIZE: H 106.7 x W 62.2 x D 69.9 cm
DESIGNER: winsor white
MANUFACTURER: pacific traders & manufacturing corp.
YEAR: 2010

This arm chair was inspired by the refined and graceful form of Chippendale furniture, which provides a perfect mix between form and function.

berna daybed

MATERIAL: rattan poles
SIZE: H 69.9 x W 259.1 x D 91.4 cm
DESIGNER: bernice montenegro
MANUFACTURER: pacific traders & manufacturing corp.
YEAR: 2010

It was the desire to give this daybed an inviting and light look that gives its the impression of simplicity in form. The straight lines with wide gaps give it a transparent quality.

anemone coffee & side tables

MATERIAL: rattan poles
SIZE: coffee table H 41.9 x Dia. 106.7 cm;
side table H 60.3 x Dia. 68.6 cm
DESIGNER: rene ybañez
MANUFACTURER: obra cebuana inc.
CLIENTS: arte primitivo
YEAR: 2010

The simple and organic design of the Anemone tables
were inspired by the designer's snorkeling adventures
and encounters with an impressive collection of
undersea creatures like the anemone, as well as the
desire to design with rattan.

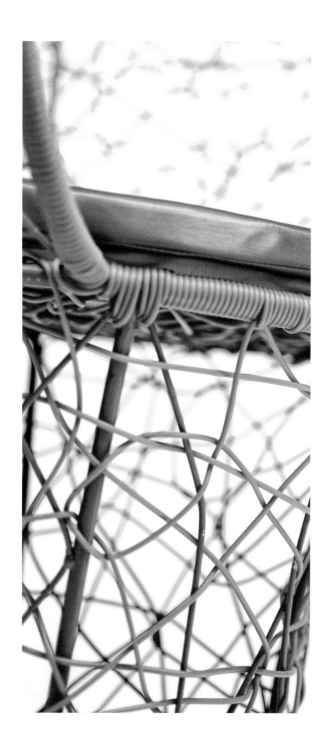

bird's nest dining chair

MATERIALS: greco polyethylene fiber materials
SIZE: H 80 x W 65 x D 54 cm
DESIGNER: marco corti
STYLISTIC VARIATIONS: living, dining, and sun-lounge pieces
MANUFACTURER: coast pacific
YEAR: 2010

The Bird's Nest Dining Chair is a light and modern chair that was inspired by the need for light and sleek but comfortable pieces; something that looks delicate but sits squarely.

This chair is a free-flowing pattern of ease and openness.

238

brook street collection
guéridon
coffee table

MATERIAL: mahogany solids
SIZE: guéridon H 73.7 x Dia 96.5 cm,
coffee table H 35.6 x W 147.3 x D 99.1 cm
MANUFACTURER: pacific traders & manufacturing corp.
YEAR: 2010

The cocktail table is reminiscent of old Hollywood glamour, this seductively low Asian-style mahogany cocktail table has dramatically scaled iconic pillar legs.

The classic guéridon is a 1940s Regency Revival-inspired occasional table with vigorously hand-carved paw feet.

tables
lamp table
cocktail table

MATERIAL: (lamp table) gmelina solids, with cherry, daniela, walnut, pine, maple quarters veneers
(cocktail table) philippine mahogany solids with cherry, daniela, walnut, pine and maple quarter veneers;
SIZE: lamp table H 66 x W 60.7 x D 60.7 x Dia. 60.1 cm; cocktail table H 63.5 x W 132.1 x D 132 cm
DESIGNER: gregg huettel
MANUFACTURER: maitland-smith
YEAR: 2010

Gregg Huettel, the designer, has always loved 'stately' columns and wanted to make a masculine showcase table for large-scale homes. The cocktail table utilizes the veneering and cabinetry skills of Maitland-Smith, as well as places a circular brass accent molding around the perimeter of the top to give it that 'wow' factor. There is even veneer inlay on the column bases themselves.

The lamp table shares the same architectural and masculine principles as the cocktail table, although the body has been reconfigured. It uses the same the veneer inlay, brass work and finish, but it has its own unique character.

The two tables combined make a bold yet harmonious statement.

commode galbée

MATERIALS: emperador stone, stingray, brass hardware, lokenai wood
SIZE: H 95 x W 49 x D 30 cm
DESIGNER: michel guinefolleau
MANUFACTURER: cebu intertrade export
YEAR: 2010

Inspired by the stylish, modern and elegant Art Deco furniture of 1922, this piece has a timeless appeal that makes it a collector's item.

cube lounge chair

MATERIALS: rattan frame with scraped rattan weaving
SIZE: H 91.4 x W 91.4 x D 91.4 cm
DESIGNER: winsor white
MANUFACTURER: pacific traders & manufacturing corp.
YEAR: 2010

The Cube Lounge Chair is a transition from rustic and organic to sleek and modern. Its inspiration was the classic lines of 1950s designs.

First scraped rattan poles

leather belt arm chair

MATERIALS: rattan frame with wicker on inner and outer back weaving and leather laminate on arms
SIZE: H 99.1 x W 60.7 x D 63.5 cm
DESIGNER: fernando "astik" villarin
MANUFACTURER: pacific traders & manufacturing corp.
YEAR: 2010

Its inspiration is an old belt that has seen better days. This piece has an unusual and striking combination of materials.

248

petals collection
end table

MATERIALS: rattan and faux shagreen top lamination
SIZE: H 50.8 x W 45.7 x D 45.7 cm
DESIGNER: bernice montenegro
MANUFACTURER: pacific traders & manufacturing corp.
YEAR: 2010

The Petals Collection End Table is a remarkable combination of materials and form that was inspired by the gentle curving form and organic appeal of petals.

philippe stack
bookshelf

MATERIALS: radiata pine, gmelina or mahogany
SIZE: H 190.5 x W 127 x D 33 cm
DESIGNER: vito selma
MANUFACTURER: stonesets international inc.
CLIENTS: george de haast, ito kish
YEAR: 2010

Little children are close to the designer's heart; this is his take on kiddie furniture. The chairs are used as interconnecting pieces to form a bookshelf that can be used for playrooms or classrooms.

The ingenuity of the multi-purpose and interlocking pieces reminds one of the French product designer, Philippe Starck.

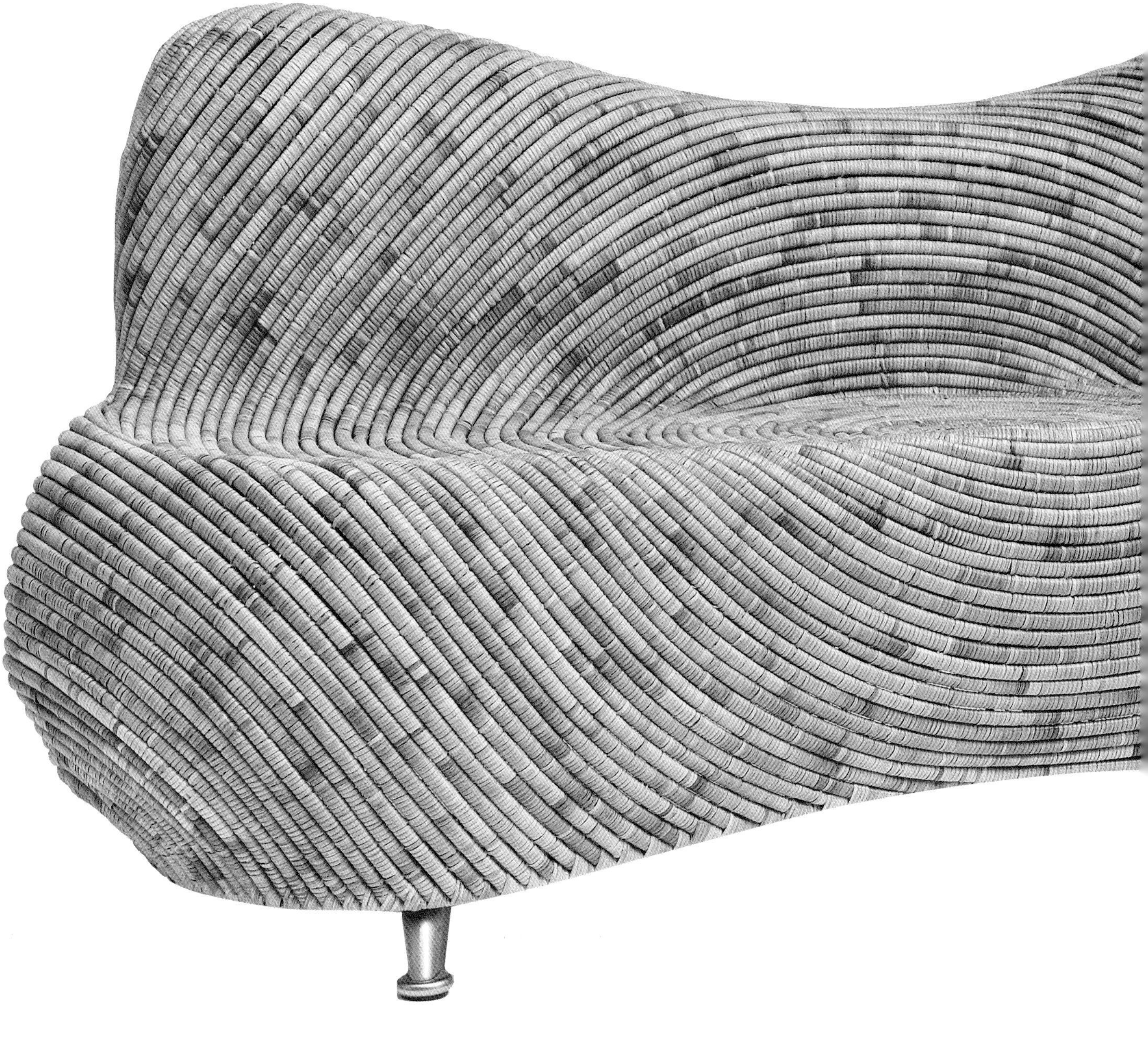

ripples

MATERIALS: rattan split woven around rattan core
SIZE: H 81 x W 181 x D 73 cm
DESIGNER: debbie palao
STYLISTIC VARIATIONS: lounge chair,
two-seater sofa (lilô sofa)
MANUFACTURER: design ventures cebu, inc.
entry to cebu next 2010
YEAR: 2010

Ripples was inspired by the concentric circles of the creamed egg whites for the lemon meringue pie the designer was baking.

sf5279 arm chair

MATERIALS: mahogany solids with bamboo strips and oak burl veneer upholstered in off-white linen fabric
SIZE: H 71.1 x W 69.9 x D 76.2 cm
DESIGNER: pride sasser
MANUFACTURER: cosonsa manufacturing, inc.
YEAR: 2010

This is a classic Art Deco-inspired arm chair interpreted with renewable bamboo inlay.

The oak burl trim of this arm chair lends a luxurious feeling in contrast to the bamboo and linen upholstery.

Crushed bamboos are laminated on wooden carcasses as a new trend in furniture design for door panels, headboards of beds and tabletops.

256

stingray lounging chair

MATERIALS: stingray and oakwood
SIZE: H 92 x W 117 x D 188 cm
DESIGNER: michel guinefolleau
MANUFACTURER: cebu intertrade export
YEAR: 2010

This Stingray Lounging Chair was inspired by the elegant, opulent, modern and often eclectic style of Art Deco furniture.

twisted lamp base

MATERIALS: stingray and wood
SIZE: H 34 x W 16 x D 16 cm
DESIGNER: michel guinefolleau
MANUFACTURER: cebu intertrade export
YEAR: 2010

The twisted lamp base was inspired by home accents in the
Art Deco style, giving it a unique, decorative and useful look.

pout chair

MATERIALS: metal, red cotton twine, hand-woven *abaca*
SIZE: H 78.6 x W 73.6 x D 54.4 cm
DESIGNER: debbie palao
MANUFACTURER: design ventures cebu, inc.
entry to cebu next 2011
YEAR: 2011

The name describes the unusual, playful shape of the chair's backrest/armrest, which curls to a "pout" when viewed sideways. Teasing and anticipating, these are what the designer, Debbie Palao, associates with travel.

The knot-weaving technique highlights the versatility and texture of cotton twine, and the vibrant, saturated shade of carmine red. Debbie Palao always seeks to highlight the natural element of all materials used in her pieces, to let these tell their story. In this case, she incorporated a weave that was not so complicated as to steal the play of curves, but one stark enough to command attention. Ergonomics is another key ingredient, besides aesthetic quality.

261

baskets
[1]market basket with handle
[2]flower basket with handle
[3]art deco basket
[4]bamboo deco flower basket

MATERIAL: 1. rattan; 2. bamboo and roots; 3. bamboo;
4. bamboo and rattan
DESIGNER: marguerite lhuillier
MANUFACTURER: infini
YEAR: 1. 1997; 2. 1998; 3. 2004; 4. 2006

Bamboo is a versatile material and its utility extends beyond being a sturdy construction material and an exquisite interweaving strip. Giant bamboo poles are used as framing for furniture. Strips of outer or inner skin are woven into furniture sidings, seats or backs.

¹chejo round bowl

MATERIALS: bamboo and rattan
DESIGNER: marguerite lhuillier
MANUFACTURER: infini
YEAR: 2004

²oriental moon sphere basket

MATERIAL: rattan
DESIGNER: marguerite lhuillier
MANUFACTURER: infini
YEAR: 2002

³bamboo splits decorative bowl

MATERIALS: bamboo and rattan
DESIGNER: marguerite lhuillier
MANUFACTURER: infini
YEAR: 2006

2

1

3

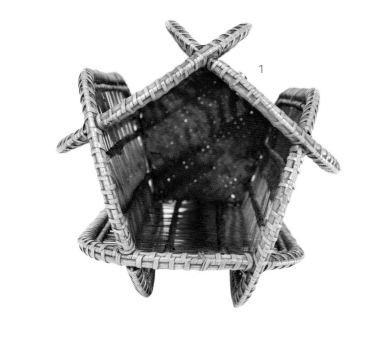

1

¹pentagon deco basket

MATERIALS: bamboo and rattan
DESIGNER: marguerite lhuillier
MANUFACTURER: infini
YEAR: 2004

²bamboo deco basket

MATERIAL: bamboo
DESIGNER: marguerite lhuillier
MANUFACTURER: infini
YEAR: 2007

2

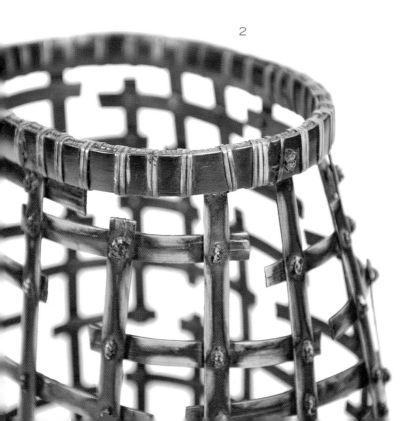

1

2

baskets

MATERIALS: 1. rattan frame with wicker and leather for the basket handles; 2. close cane with skin; 3. scraped rattan weaving
DESIGNER: pilar streegan
MANUFACTURER: pacific traders & manufacturing corp.
YEAR: 2010

These baskets by Pilar Streegan were inspired by organic and geometric forms, giving the impression of simplicity.

1

2

3

baskets

MATERIALS: rattan frame with sliced rattan
and *abaca* weaving
DESIGNER: bernice montenegro
MANUFACTURER: pacific traders & manufacturing corp.
YEAR: 2010

Simple and organic, these baskets were inspired by
the lowly chicken basket.

1

2

3

afterword

Cebu's furniture industry enjoyed decades of prosperity, steadily growing from a cottage industry into a major contributor to the Philippine economy. From a handful of enterprising individuals in the 1950s to hundreds of manufacturers employing thousands of skilled workers in the 1990s, it has gone through expected twists and turns.

Cebu's industry players recognized a need to organize themselves to deal with common concerns that went with development and growth. With its ranks increasing rapidly, Cebu's membership in the Chamber of Furniture Industries of the Philippines (CFIP) as a chapter was insufficient to address the myriad of issues that affected local businesses focused primarily on export.

In 1974, the Cebu Furniture Industries Foundation, Inc. (CFIF, Inc.), composed of manufacturers, traders and subcontractors of furniture and furnishings, was formed. Envisioned as a business organization whose primary objective is to provide industry support for its members, it actively engages in programs designed to improve productivity and market development. Among its many projects is the 22-year old Cebu International Furniture and Furnishings Exhibition, an international trade show recognized and attended by major furniture buyers worldwide. Known for years as Cebu X, it now goes by the name Cebu NEXT, boldly positioning itself as a key resource for defining global furniture trends.

The Cebu furniture industry faces many challenges today as it matures; as it meets failures and successes that create an invaluable roadmap to achieving higher degrees of excellence and fortune. Its dependence on the U.S. market, up to a high of 70%

of total exports, has turned boon years into bane. The major downturn of the U.S. economy and subsequently other global economies has hurt many of the exporters, shutting down plants and bringing on the demise of businesses. China, Vietnam and Indonesia have made serious dents in traditional markets, forcing the Cebu Furniture industry to recognize its strong competitors in the region. To those who remain committed to furniture manufacturing, however, these are difficulties that need to be hurdled and overcome.

These are interesting times and as the industry struggles to reinvent itself into Southeast Asia's design center. The success of Cebu's furniture industry, while partly attributable to history, local culture and geography, is tied to a strong entrepreneurial spirit and a creative sense that knows no boundaries. It is people with furniture in their blood that will take the industry to new heights.

The CFIF office in Jagobiao, Cebu

CEBU FURNITURE INDUSTRIES FOUNDATION

The Cebu Furniture Industries Foundation, Inc. (CFIF, Inc.) is the primary industry support organization of furniture manufacturers and exporters in the Philippines.

It is the voice of the country's furniture export industry and also serves as its rationalizing body. Through its developmental efforts, CFIF provides a venue for discussion and resolution of industry – related issues.

Established in 1974, CFIF is envisioned as a support organization to Cebu's furniture industry, strengthening cooperation among members and responding to the needs of the industry's international markets and to make the Philippine Furniture Industry the leader of high-quality, design-oriented furniture and furnishings in Southeast Asia.

CFIF links the industry to the global market place. It is the only furniture organization in the Philippines that bridges its members with the world.

PROJECT GREEN MOUNTAIN, BLUE SEA

As the primary support organization of the furniture industry, the Cebu Furniture Industries Foundation, Inc. (CFIF) serves as catalyst of all aspects of development in the sector, including building a good image of the industry through corporate social responsibility (CSR).

To encourage member-companies to practice CSR, CFIF launched in 1997 the project, Green Mountain, Blue Sea. The project aims to raise awareness among member-companies to participate and practice good environmental stewardship and social accountability.

Since the task of institutionalizing CSR is an ambitious one, CFIF partnered with the Philippine Business for Social Progress (PBSP) and Ocean Care Advocates to implement the project.

With Project Green Mountain, Blue Sea, CFIF adopted 19 hectares of upland reforestation parks in Cebu's watersheds and five hectares of mangrove in Olango Island where a protected bird sanctuary is located.

Under the project, CFIF and its partners organize annual upland and coastal tree planting activities, as well as coastal clean-up drives, with the participation of owners and employees of member companies.

Apart from the project's activities, CFIF also integrated CSR awareness into different trainings and seminars.

Project Green Mountain, Blue Sea and other special projects are conducted by CFIF every year also to enhance camaraderie and build stronger relationship among member – companies, industry players and partners.

The CSR ideals in these projects give camaraderie-building in the organization more meaning.

CEBU NEXT

CEBU NEXT, previously known as Cebu X, is the 22-year old Cebu International Furnishings Exhibition organized by CFIF.

As CEBU NEXT, the exhibition embodies the drive to create new designs with exceptional quality. It harnesses and consolidates the collective strength of the Philippine furniture industry, while highlighting Cebu as the design capital of Southeast Asia.

Cebu has a rich history in furniture making. So rich that is even the key source for trends that are followed worldwide, such as the popularity of rattan and *buri* in the 60s and 70s respectively, stone craft in the 80's, cane and iron furnishings in the 90's and the *abaca* trend of early 2000. CEBU NEXT continues this leading legacy by setting its sights forward to the furniture trends of the coming decade.

KAGIKAN: RETURN TO THE SOURCE

Furniture pieces made and designed in Cebu have become well noted for their fresh concepts, innovative construction and radical choice of materials. Cebuano furniture, in particular, is widely regarded for using ethnic-based inspirations executed into designs with global appeal.

Prior to Magellan's discovery in the year 1521, Cebu was a meeting ground for various Asian races congregating in mutual and beneficial trade. In those times, it was common to find Indonesian farmers, Malaysian craftsmen, Chinese artisans, Arab spice dealers, and Indian ware-merchants exchanging goods, services and ideas which has made Cebu the multi-cultural melting pot that it is today.

For the CEBU NEXT 2011, the Cebu Furniture Industries Foundation (CFIF) launched the Kagikan Project, a collaboration of noted designers based around the world, all tied together by a common heritage, and by their membership in EPOCH, an organization of designers, whose aim is to promote care for the environment through ecologically sustainable designs. EPOCH is a fusion of young talented artists and designers setting a benchmark for the very best in contemporary Filipino Art & Design, with a regard for avant garde.

The expo's theme was "Crossing Cultures", an examination of how the influence of global ethnicities has developed the Cebuano designers' cultural identity. The expo hopes to convey how an exploration of one's roots from within the Philippines and throughout the whole world brings a fresh perspective and an uncommon point of view.

Five designers from EPOCH participated in the Kagikan project, namely Daniel Latorre-Cruz (London, England), Martha Cech (Vienna, Austria), Wataru Sakuma (U.S.), Jinggoy Buensuceso (Singapore) and Stanley Ruiz (New York, U.S.).

EPOCH exhibited innovative furniture and products with the emphasis of using sustainable materials at the expo. Each designer was paired with a furniture company to manufacture high quality showpieces. Both the designer and the manufacturer worked together, combining the former's artistic identity and the latter's craftsmanship, to come up with a unique and modern final showpiece.

Opposite page:
Top photo, clockwise from back: Split Chair by Daniel Latorre Cruz for Casa Cebuana Incorporada; Rebaroque Table by Wataru Sakuma for Stonesets International Inc.; Bubbles Coffee Table by Martha Cech for Cebu Natura Crafts, Phils., Inc.; Secret Stone by Daniel Latorre Cruz for Stonesets International Inc.; Brown Pandora Baskets by Stanley Ruiz for Hacienda Crafts Company, Inc.; Drum Wireframe Table by Stanley Ruiz for Crafters of Cebu, Inc.

Bottom, left: Red Doodle Chair by Jinggoy Buensuceso for Heritage Muebles Mirabile Export, Inc.

Bottom, right: Ribbon Chair by Wataru Sakuma for Tadeco Incorporated

This page:
LUPA by Jinggoy Buensuceso and Crisma Hope Gabasa for Cebu Natura Crafts, Phils., Inc. (above); Rebaroque Chair by Wataru Sakuma for Stonesets International Inc. (right)

photo timeline

1920s 1959 1968 1968 1970s 1970s

1970 1975 1978 1979 1979 1980s

1980s 1980s 1981 1983 1985 1985

1986 1990 1993 1993 1995 1995

1995 1995 1997 1997 1997 1998

1998 1999 1999 1999 1999 2000

2000 2000 2000 2000 2000 2000

2000 2000 2001 2002 2002 2002

2003 2003 2003 2003 2003 2003

2004 2004 2004 2004 2004 2004

2004	2005	2005	2005	2005	2005
2005	2005	2006	2006	2006	2006
2006	2007	2007	2007	2007	2007
2007	2007	2007	2007	2007	2007
2007	2007	2007	2008	2008	2008
2008	2008	2008	2008	2008	2008

index

A

abaca 44, 65
abaca rope 132
abaca weave 123
Aboitiz, Doña Maria 20, 22-24, 27, 30
Aboitiz, Josephine, 22, 27-28
Afra e Tobia Scarpa 100
agates 188
Alegrado, Arcadio 54
Alegrado, Eduardo 52, 54
Alenter Cane Corporation 41, 52-54
Allied Stores 63
aluminum 82
Amadeus occasional table (set of 2) ambulante style 212-213
ancient Chinese raincoat with stand 170
anemone coffee and side tables 234-235
Anja collection 90-91
Apy Cane Incorporated 136, 139, 209
Arden Classic Inc. 130
arm chair 26-27, 45, 62, 153, 160, 230-231, 246-247
      model 5505 52
      sf5279 254-255
Armoire 146-147
Arrolado, Mae 17
Arroyo, Gloria Macapagal 64
art deco basket 262
Arte Primitivo (Mexico) 235
Artistica 229
Atelier'a 115
Atillo Manufacturing Corp. (AMANCOR) 31, 62-64
Atillo, Florentino 27, 30, 31, 62, 63
Atillo, Florentino III 31, 62-64
Atillo, Irma 31, 63-64
Atillo, Melissa 64
Atillo, Narcisa 30-31

Atillo's House of Rattan 30
Atillo's Rattan and Wood Industries, Inc. 30-31

B

B&B Italia 100-101, 106-109, 174-175, 200-201
bamboo 44, 263
Bamboo collection 78-79
bamboo deco basket 264-265
bamboo deco flower basket 262
bamboo polymer deco 170
bamboo splits decorative bowl 263
bandana occasional chair 148-149
Barilone, Maurice 115
basket, detail of 48
baskets 262-267
basquet 51
Batuka 199
Baud bench 172-173
Bayern Munich 82
beds 128-129, 138-139, 156-157
Belleza, Charles 88-89
Berna daybed 232-233
Bilibid chair 20-21
bird's nest dining chair 236-237
Black, John 228-229
bloom lounge chair 218-219
Board of Investments 53
Bon-Ace Fashion Tools, Inc. 162, 171
Bonacina Pierantonio 24
Bonet, Antonio 142
Bonghanoy, Ramir 162, 171
Booth, Josephine Aboitiz 23, 27, 41
Booth, Robert 29
Borders 50
brain tanning 107
Brook Street collection 238-239

Bubbles coffee table 274-275
Buensuceso, Jinggoy 273-275
buffalo leather 107
buntal 38
Bureau of Customs 53
buri 38
buri furniture 38, 54
butterfly chair 41, 142-143
Butuan 63
Buzon, Giovanne 91

C

camp chair 143
canasta circular sofa 175
canasta sofa 174
capiz shell floor lamp 85
        detail of 85
capiz shells 176
Casa Cebuana 32-33, 111, 117, 154-155, 275
Casquejo, Pat 61
Castilex Industrial Corporation 38, 61-62, 82-83, 126, 143, 169
Castillo, Guido 61
cat-tail 167
CCIC 73
Cebu 9-10, 15, 20, 70, 74, 83
        furniture industry 17, 44
        history 13
Cebu Design Education Foundation (CDEF) 84-85
Cebu Fil-veneer 115
Cebu Furniture Designers Guild 84
Cebu Furniture Global Gallery 97
Cebu Furniture Industries Foundation, Inc. (CFIF, Inc.) 7, 84
Cebu Intertrade Export 243, 257-258
Cebu Natura Crafts, Phils., Inc. 274-275
Cebu NEXT 7, 253, 261, 268, 272
Cebu School of Arts and Trade 30

Cebu X 6, 169, 268, 272
Cebuano workforce 74
Cech, Martha 273-275
Centerpiece Collection 130-131
Central Bank of the Philippines 53
Chairs 20-21, 24-27, 39-41, 45, 51-52, 56-57, 60-61, 97-99, 112,
        121-122, 132-133, 136-138, 142-143, 148-149, 153, 160,
        162, 178-181, 184-185, 192-193, 218-221, 228-31, 236-237,
        244-247, 254-257, 260-261
Chamber of Furniture Industries of the Philippines (CFIP)
        41, 60
Chejo round bowl 263
Chelsea House 163
chest 214-217
China 44, 64, 72, 83
Christianson, Bernard 186, 217
Citterio, Antonio 107, 108
Classical Geometry 118, 203
Claudia sofa 104-105
Climaco, Agustin 62, 82
Coast Pacific 97, 236-237
Cobonpue, Betty 56, 58, 102-103
Cobonpue, Kenneth 4, 9, 60, 84, 120-121, 123, 132-133, 150,
        152-153, 156-157, 159, 184-185, 218-219
coffee table 88, 102-103, 114-115, 118-119, 132, 151, 161-162,
        196-197, 234, 239
Collezione Basilan 1 100-101
commode galbée 242-243
console cabinet with matching mirror frame 176-177
console mosaic table 86-87
console table 28-29, 144-145, 164-165, 186-187, 191, 198-199
Corporate Social Responsibility (CSR) 270-271
Corti, Marco 236
Corypha elata Roxb. 38
Cosonsa Manufacturing, Inc. 78, 254
cracked ice chair 40

Crafters of Cebu, Inc. 274-275, 298
craftsmanship 9, 17, 33, 38, 51, 74
creativity 74
Crimson Resort and Spa lobby 8-9, 11
Crisanto, Joseph 208-209
Croissant collection
       coffee table & end table 132
       easy arm chair 132-133
Cruz, Alice Streegan 50
Cruz, Daniel Latorre 273-275
cube lounge chair 244-245
Curate home collection 228-229
cutgrass vase 140

D

daybed 154-155
daydream 134-135
DEDON 82-83, 135, 141
      Fiber 135
Dekeyser, Bobby 82, 83
Delantar, Catherine 89
Delantar, Pedro Herrera Jr. 89, 91
Delos Santos, Maria Luisa 84
demography 15
Department of Finance 53
design innovations 84
Design Today 86
Design Ventures Cebu, Inc. 196, 221, 253, 261
designers 84-85
Detalia Aurora Inc 140, 179, 207, 213
dining table 56, 86, 121, 123-125, 196, 206-207
Ditzel, Nanna 24
dragon's tail lamps
      floor lamp 210
      hanging lamp 211
Drum Wireframe Table 274-275

E

egg chair 24-25
Eisen, Leonard 112
Elite 118
encomiendas 14
end table 103, 121, 132, 163, 184, 196, 248-249
EPOCH 273

Ernest Hemingway® collection 126-129
      bar stool 126-127
      stand-up desk 126-127
      kilimanjaro bed 128-129
Ethan Allen 145
exports 53

F

Ferrari-Hardoy, Jorge 142
Ficks Reed Rattan 30
Figueroa, Guillermo 32-33, 53
Figueroa-Paulin, Angela 33
Florentino III International Inc. (F3) 64
flower basket with handle 262
Forbes, Eleanor 24
Frinier, Richard 83, 135, 141
Furniture industry 6-7, 9, 12, 17, 33, 44, 56, 68, 74, 84, 89
      mixed media in 53

G

Gabasa, Crisma Hope 275
Gamallo, Othello 38, 65
Gamallo, Quirico 39, 61-62, 65, 98
Gamallosons Traders, Inc. 39, 65, 98
gantang 136
gantang corner chair 136
gantang side chair 136-137
Garry Masters 31
gemstone fish 188-189
George de Haast (South Africa) 250
Globe West (Australia) 172
Go, Ronnie Fernando 176
gold fish with stone base 158
Golden Shell Award 33, 49
Gonzales, Tony 225
Gorsia Design Pvt. Ltd. 203
Gothic architecture 28
Gothic Movement 28
Grandwood Furniture 72
Green Mountain, Blue Sea 270-271
Greigo bed and night stand 139
Greigo II side chair 138
Guinefolleau, Michel 4, 243, 257-258
Gushurst, Clarence 20

H

Hacienda Crafts Company, Inc. 274-275, 298
halo lamp 159

Hanako cocktail table 190-191
Heritage Muebles Mirabile Export, Inc. 274-275
Hemingway, Ernest 126, 129
Henredon 73
Hive 150, 159, 195, 210, 222
Huettel, Gregg 145, 163, 183, 186, 214, 217, 240
Huin, Alain 111

I

Infini 158, 170, 262-264
Insular Bank of Cebu 49
Interior Crafts of the Islands Inc. 56, 58, 60, 103, 121, 123, 132, 153, 156, 184, 218
Ipong, Rey G. 117, 154
Ito Kish (Philippine distributor) 172, 191, 250

J

JCL Export Inc. 176

K

Kai floor lamp 150
kamansi 151
Kandinsky coffee table 114-115
Kilimanjaro bed 128-129
Kim3 (U.S.) 122
Kurchan, Juan 142

L

La Villa del Santisimo Nombre de Jesus 14
lamp 30, 49, 71, 78, 85, 150, 159, 195, 210-211, 222-225, 258-259, 298
    lamp table 240
lampakanay 167
Lampert, Hervé 83
Lampert, Vince 83
lasang side chair 192-193
lauan 86
Laxina, Joseph 195
leather belt arm chair 246-247
leather-wrapped book cocktail table 68-69
Legazpi, Miguel Lopez de 14
Lhuillier, Marguerite 158, 170, 262-264
Ligthart, Frank 81, 83
Linea Fina 29
Longhorn occasional chair 178-179
Longhorn ottoman 178-179
Lopez, Narcisa 30-31
lost wax process 71

lounge chairs 16, 63, 81, 162, 218-221, 244-245, 253
Lux suspension lamp 194-195

M

Mactan Economic Zone 70
Maduzia, Bernie 38
Magellan, Ferdinand 13, 272
Magellan Veneer Corporation 50
maharajah chair 38-39
Maitland-Smith Cebu Inc. 68, 70-71, 124, 146, 240
Maitland-Smith Limited 70, 240
Maitland-Smith Philippines Inc. (MSPI) 70
Maitland-Smith, Paul 68, 72-73, 78
Mandalay console table 164-165
Mandaue Galleon Trade 65
Manguerra, Christy 222
Manufacturing 6, 9-10, 12-13, 29, 37, 44
Marcos, Ferdinand 31
market basket with handle 262
Marmorcast 91
Massaud, Jean-Marie 83
maze coffee table 196-197
McGuire "bamboo" table 9
McGuire Furniture Company 20, 23, 24, 27-28, 38, 41, 42, 45, 180
McGuire rattan arm chairs 9
McGuire, Elinor 9, 22-24, 27-28, 38, 40, 42, 45
McGuire, John 9, 22-23, 27-28, 38, 42, 45, 180
Mehitabel Furniture Inc. 20, 24, 27-30, 38, 40-42, 45, 122, 129, 160-161
Mendco 112
Meryll 220-221
Metal furniture manufacturing 65, 71, 73
micro-mosaic 89
Mindanao Rattan Corporation 41-42, 53
Minor, Janice 188, 199
Montenegro, Bernice 49, 84, 105, 149, 204,233, 249, 267
mosaic 86-88
mosaic process 89
mother of pearl shell dish 70-71
Museum of Modern Art (New York) 27

N

Nature's Legacy Eximport, Inc. 89-91
Naturescast® 89, 91
Navone, Paola 86
Nejar, Alain 88
Nguyen, Toan 83

Nixon, Richard 9
Norkis Trading 41, 53
Nuebo Tienda (Dominican Republic) 122, 160-161

O

O'Asian 30
obelisk 80-81
Obra Cebuana Inc. 164, 235
Ocean Care Advocates 271
Ocean's 13 9
Oggetti 199
Orbit 141
oriental moon sphere basket 263
Othello two-seater sofa 168-169
Ovium collection mirror 171

P

Pacific Traders & Manufacturing Corp. 41, 49-51, 53, 100,
        105, 107-108, 142, 145, 149, 151, 166, 175, 180, 183,
        186, 192, 200, 204, 214, 217, 226, 229-230, 233,
        239, 244, 246, 249
Padilla, Val 85
Palao, Debbie 84, 196, 221, 253, 261
Palasan dining set 42-43
Pampanga 37
Pandora Baskets 274-275
peacock chairs 61, 98-99
pentagon deco basket 264-265
Petals collection end table 248-249
petrified wood 199
petrified wood console table 198-199
Philippe stack bookshelf 250-251
Philippine Bureau of Patents, Trademarks and
        Technology Transfer 88
Philippine Business for Social Progress (PBSP) 271
Philippines 9-11, 13, 20, 37, 64, 83, 86
Piazza San Marco 88
Pier 1 Imports 38, 61-63, 65
Pigalle 123
Pitt, Brad 9
planter (banana leaf collection) 166-167
Politecnico Internazionale di Architettura e Design 49
poppy lamps 222-223
        floor lamp 223
        hanging lamp 222
pout chair 260-261
princess chair 38, 98
Project Kagikan 272-273

R

raffia 38
Raphael Legacy Designs Inc. 86, 88, 225
rattan 22-24, 27, 29-30, 37, 41, 44, 50, 54, 60, 62-63, 68, 70,
        82-83, 86, 89, 111
        and metal 73
        furniture 9, 20, 22-24, 27, 29-30, 32-33, 37, 41,
                53-54, 62-63, 72, 88
        poles 12, 32-33, 37, 41, 49-50, 53-55, 88
        suppliers 41
Rattan Originals, Inc. 32-33
rattan target (TM) arm chair 45
ravel 200-201
rawhide binding 22-24
Reagan, Ronald 9
Rebaroque chair 275
Rebaroque table 274-275
Red Brown (Australia) 191
Red Doodle Chair 274-275
Reunion Furnishings Inc. 53
Ribbon Chair 274-275
ribbon coffee table 102-103
ripples 252-253
Robb & Stucky (U.S.) 160-161
Roberts, Albert 72
Robinson, Luisa 140, 179, 207, 210
Rodriguez, Paula 213
Ruiz, Stanley 273-275, 298

S

S-4 108-109
S-5 106-107
Sakuma, Wataru 273-275
Safari camp chair 142
salbaro bench table 202-203
Santo Niño 13-14
Sasser, Pride 70, 73, 78, 254
Secret Stone 274-275
Selma, Vito 172, 191, 250
settee 110-111
Shattuck, Howard 73
shipping 10
Siarot, Arden 130
side chair, model 5500 52
slatted walnut chair 180-181
snowman hanging lamp 224-225
solehiya weaving on Manhattan Hassock, detail of 97
South Korea 72

284

Spain 15, 53
St. Mark's Basilica 88
St. Tropez 112-113
    chair 112
    table 113
Standard Rattan 41, 53
Standard Vacuum Oil 22
star storage 208-209
stingray lounging chair 256-257
Stonecast 89, 91
Stonecraft 88
Stonesets International Inc. 172, 191, 250, 275
Streegan, Gorgonia 49-50
Streegan, Hugo Jr. 49-50
Streegan, Pilar 49, 266
Streep, Meryll 221
Sugbu
    city 13
    table 226-227
sushi lounge chair 17
    detail of 16
swirl side table 204-205

T

table 9, 37-38, 42-43, 50, 68, 80-81, 86-88, 100, 102-103, 112-
    113, 115, 118, 124, 132, 139, 144-145, 151, 164, 182-183,
    186-187, 190-191, 196-197, 199-200, 202-205, 212-213,
    226-227, 234-235, 238-239, 240-241, 248-249, 254, 275
Tai Chong 30
Tanseco, Carlo S. 169
Thailand 73, 83
Thatcher, Margaret 9
Theodore and Alexander 73
Thomasville Furniture 126, 129
Tilt collection
    arm chair 153
    sofa 152-153
tindalo 13
tortola sofa 116-117
Totong coffee table 151
tourism 10
tray table 182-183
Tugonon, Clayton 118, 202-203
Tugonon, Seth 88
Tuscan coffee table, detail of 88
Tuskany 206-207
    console 207
    dining table 206-207

Tuttle, Edward 41
twisted lamp base 258-259

U

University of the Philippines (Cebu campus) 84
Urquiola, Patricia 175, 200

V

Varona chair, detail of 97
Varya Home Designs (India) 172, 191
Veloso, Antonio 62
Veloso, Michael 62
venetta egg-shaped coffee table 118-119
Vietnam 73, 269
Villarin, Fernando "Astik" 1, 4, 96-97, 151, 166-167, 192-193,
    226-227, 246-247
Voyage collection 2, 4, 156-157
    bed 156-157
    day bed 2, 4

W

Web collection
    lounge chair 162
    two-seater chair 162
Weylandts 118, 203
White, Winsor 73, 122, 124, 146, 160-161, 230, 244
wicker 104
    furniture 50, 82
Wicker & Vine, Inc. 163
Williams, Shelby 52
Wimbledon 9
wing back chair 122
Wistehuff, Daniel Sr. 126, 129
Worldmark Furniture Industries, Inc. 50

Y

Ybañez, Rene 84, 97, 164-165, 234-235
yin & yang
    arm chair 121
    sofa 120
Yoda 184-185
Yu, Corito Escario 84, 136, 139
Yu, Julie 139
Yu, Noreen 139
Yu, Tony 73

Z

z-mat 169, 183

photo credits

irma atillo
31, 62

bim bacaltos
watercolor renditions
26, 29, 45 (left)

josephine booth
23

medal elepaño
8, 11-13, 15, 34-36, 48, 65-67, 75, 85
(right), 92-93, 104 (inset), 111 (inset),
149, 183 (inset), 244 (inset), 254 (inset),
263 (inset)

gregg huettel
144, 163, 182, 187, 215-216, 240-241

ted madamba
4, 14, 20-21, 39, 52, 61, 71, 82, 86-88, 90,
96-97, 99, 104-105, 110-113, 116-119, 122,
126-131, 134, 141, 143, 148, 151, 154-155,
158, 160-162, 164-173, 176-179, 181, 189-
193, 196-199, 202-203, 205, 207, 212-
213, 220-221, 224-227, 230-239, 242-243,
245-249, 251-253, 255-256, 259, 262-267

graham maitland-smith
69, 72

patricia mancao
16, 18-19, 46-47, 76-77, 132 (inset), 169
(inset), 188 (inset), 199 (inset)

luisa robinson
140, 206

alenter cane/
ambiente designs international inc.
55

apy cane incorporated
136-139, 208-209

artistica
229

b&b italia
100-101, 106, 108-109, 174-175, 201

casa cebuana incorporada
32

cebu fil-veneer corporation
114

cfif
6-7, 269, 274-275

citem
167 (inset), 176 (inset)

cosonsa manufacturing, inc.
79

dedon manufacturing inc.
80-81

dekeyser & friends
135 (inset)

design ventures cebu, inc.
260-261

interior crafts of the islands inc.
2-3, 57-60, 102-103, 120-121, 123, 132-133, 150, 152-153, 157, 159, 184-185, 194, 210-211, 218-219, 222-223

maitland-smith cebu
124-125, 147

mcguire furniture company
27-28, 40-41, 45 (right)

mehitabel furniture inc.
24-25, 42-43

pacific traders &
manufacturing corp.
1, 50-51, 85 (left), 107 (inset), 142, 228

cfif directory

accessoria inc.
Corner Sitio Bagacay and Tawagan, Tayud
Consolacion 6001, Cebu
TEL: (6332) 424.6551
FAX: (6332) 345.4680; 424.6551
EMAIL: marketing@accessoriainc.com
WEBSITE: www.accessoriainc.com

aileen's craft manufacturing
M.L. Quezon National Highway, Brgy. Mactan
Lapu-Lapu 6015, Cebu
TEL: (6332) 238.8390
FAX: (6332) 495.7968
EMAIL: info@comfortmod.com;
jackie_comfortmod@yahoo.com

ambiente designs international inc.
P.L. Sanchez St., Brgy. Tingub, Mandaue 6014, Cebu
TEL: (6332) 236.4233
FAX: (6332) 343.9155
EMAIL: csg@ambiente-designs.com
WEBSITE: www.ambiente-designs.com

amcha multi-purpose cooperative
Sitio Aleth, Cabitoonan, Toledo City 6038, Cebu
TEL: (6332) 322.5598
FAX: (6332) 322.5598
EMAIL: amcha_coop@yahoo.com.ph

angel whispers gifts and crafts
Warehouse 2 Sabalex Cmpd. Diamond St., Lahug 6000, Cebu
TEL: (6332) 232.6275; 412.2370
FAX: (6332) 231.4841
EMAIL: angelwhispersgiftsandcrafts@yahoo.com;
c23_143@yahoo.com
WEBSITE: www.angelwhispers.com

antonio bryan development corporation
Zone Pechay, Pakna-an, Mandaue City, Cebu
TEL: (6332) 346.8871; 420.4641
FAX: (6332) 346.1581
EMAIL: abdc@pldtdsl.net
WEBSITE: www.antoniobryan.com

apy cane incorporated
S.E. Jayme St., Pakna-an, Mandaue 6014, Cebu
TEL: (6332) 420.4360
FAX: (6332) 343.9183
EMAIL: info@apycane.com
WEBSITE: www.apycane.com

arden classic inc.
Soong II, Mactan, Lapu-Lapu 6015, Cebu
TEL: (6332) 238.5962-63; 495.8328
FAX: (6332) 495.8328
EMAIL: marketing@ardenclassic.com;
ardencls@yahoo.com
WEBSITE: www.ardenclassic.com

arkwell international corporation
Washington St., Basak, Lapu-Lapu 6015, Cebu
TEL: (6332) 340.2320; 340.4472

FAX: (6332) 340.4474
EMAIL: arkwell@arkwell.ph;
darlene@arkwell.ph
WEBSITE: www.arkwell.com

asian vine furniture
Basak Road, Lapu-Lapu 6015, Cebu
TEL: (6332) 341.0257; 495.6628
FAX: (6332) 341.0258
EMAIL: gvb@asianvinefurniture.com.ph
WEBSITE: www.asianvinefurniture.com.ph

axent wood corporation
Cadi Compound, Hernan Cortes St., Banilad,
Mandaue 6014, Cebu
TEL: (6332) 345.0401 to 03
FAX: (6332) 346.0857
EMAIL: axent@axentwood.com
WEBSITE: www.axentwood.com

berben wood industries, inc.
Sacris Road Ext., Tipolo, Mandaue 6014, Cebu
TEL: (6332) 346.5471 to 75
FAX: (6332) 346.0181
EMAIL: info@berbenwood.com;
enrison@berbenwood.com
WEBSITE: www.berbenwood.com

bon-ace fashion tools, inc.
Tungkil, Minglanilla 6046, Cebu
TEL: (6332) 273.7887 to 88

FAX: (6332) 273.7889
EMAIL: info@bon-ace.com;
sales@bon-ace.com;
marketing@bon-ace.com
WEBSITE: www.bon-ace.com

brianex cane, inc.
301 Legazpi St., Cebu
TEL: (6332) 253.8777; 253.0093; 346.5591 (factory)
FAX: (6332) 255.2505
EMAIL: edmund@filmonhardware.com

c.c. ex-imp, inc.
Basak, Mandaue 6014, Cebu
TEL: (6332) 345.3058; 346.0354; 345.3058
FAX: (6332) 346.0354; 345.1061
EMAIL: ccxm@mozcom.com

casa caña, inc.
Casa Washington St., Cansojong, Talisay 6045, Cebu
TEL: (6332) 272.7649
FAX: (6332) 272.7649
EMAIL: casacana@pldtdsl.net;
casacanainc@yahoo.com

casa cebuana incorporada
Tangke, Talisay 6045, Cebu
TEL: (6332) 272.3557 to 59; 491.9292
FAX: (6332) 272.3550
EMAIL: info@casacebuana.com
WEBSITE: www.casacebuana.com

castilex industrial corporation
Brgy. Tingub, Mandaue City, Cebu
TEL: (6332) 422.2050; 422.2060
FAX: (6332) 343.9155
EMAIL: csg@ambiente-designs.com

castilex trading corporation
M.L. Quezon St. Cabangcalan, Mandaue 6014, Cebu
TEL: (6332) 345.0026
FAX: (6332) 345.0026
EMAIL: sales.trading@castilex.com

castlebrook international corporation
Tungkop, Minglanilla 6046, Cebu
TEL: (6332) 272.8495
FAX: (6332) 272.8497
EMAIL: lisa_bruce_cic@yahoo.com.ph;
castlebrook_intl_corp@yahoo.com.ph

catalina embroideries, inc.
Upper Tingub, Mandaue 6014, Cebu
TEL: (6332) 346.2829
FAX: (6332) 346.2828
EMAIL: jls@catalina.ph
WEBSITE: www.catalina.ph

catarman industries inc.
Sitio Dapdap, Catarman
Lilo-an 6002, Cebu
TEL: (6332) 424.6337-38
FAX: (6332) 424.6339
EMAIL: ciicbu@gmail.com

cebu fil-veneer corporation
Gate # 2 MEPZ I, Lapu-Lapu 6015, Cebu
TEL: (6332) 340.0301; 340.0303

FAX: (6332) 340.0287
EMAIL: cordaro@filveneer.com
WEBSITE: www.filveneer.com

cebu intertrade export
693 M. L. Quezon St., Casuntingan, Mandaue 6014, Cebu
TEL: (6332) 346.3952
FAX: (6332) 343.6454
EMAIL: gacite@skyinet.net;
gacite@pldtdsl.net

cebu natura crafts, phils., inc.
Hernan Cortes St., Mandaue 6014, Cebu
TEL: (6332) 345.1908; 416.1890
FAX: (6332) 345.3842
EMAIL: cebunatura@yahoo.com.ph

celloom furniture corporation
10H Abellana St., Canduman, Mandaue 6014, Cebu
TEL: (6332) 238.843; 422.1127 loc 116
FAX: (6332) 343.9005 loc 115
EMAIL: rvillamor@celloom-ph.com
WEBSITE: www.celloom-ph.com

chikai international corporation
Suico-Du Comp., Tabok, Mandaue 6014, Cebu
TEL: (6332) 422.9896 to 97
FAX: (6332) 422.9897
EMAIL: chikaidesigns@yahoo.com.ph

christone industries
C.P. Batiller St., Umapad, Mandaue 6014, Cebu
TEL: (6332) 344.0596; 328.4050
FAX: (6332) 344.5271
EMAIL: chris@cstoneind.com
WEBSITE: www.christone.net

clarson enterprises, Inc.
Door #4 DISPO Philippines Building, A.C. Cortes
Avenue, Cambaro, Mandaue 6014, Cebu
TEL: (6332) 346.0512; 346.4596; 344.5696
FAX: (6332) 346.0512
EMAIL: cffruelda@acflogistics.com
WEBSITE: www.clarsonexport.com

classical geometry export trading
Tingub, Riverside Pagsabungan,
Mandaue 6014, Cebu
TEL: (6332) 422.1415; 343.9691
FAX: (6332) 238.1004
EMAIL: classicalgeometry@gmail.com
WEBSITE: www.classicalgeometry.com

comparts industries, inc.
S. Jayme St., Zone Tamatis Pakna-an,
Mandaue 6014, Cebu
TEL: (6332) 344.3925; 346.2111
FAX: (6332) 346.2111
EMAIL: jane@comparts.ph.com;
comparts@comparts.ph.com
WEBSITE: www.comparts.ph.com

classicware ex-import co., inc.
Lower Calajo-an, Minglanilla 6046, Cebu
TEL: (6332) 273.8778
FAX: (6332) 273.8778
EMAIL: classicware@gmail.com

clear export industries, inc.
Mabugat Road Tabok, Mandaue 6014, Cebu
TEL: (6332) 346.6852 to 54
FAX: (6332) 346.0887
EMAIL: mktg@clearex.com.ph

coast pacific manufacturing corp.
Coast Pacific St., Mahiga Creek, Kasambagan,
Banilad 6000, Cebu
TEL: (6332) 231.4277; 231.4301
FAX: (6332) 231.4301
EMAIL: info@coast-pacific.com; coastp@mozcom.com
WEBSITE: www.coast-pacific.com;
www.furniturespecialistinc.com

cosonsa manufacturing, inc.
G. Ouano St., Alang-Alang, Mandaue 6014, Cebu
TEL: (6332) 346.5090; 345.3958
FAX: (6332) 420.3506
EMAIL: cosonsa@gmail.com; esg.cosonsa@gmail.com

crafters of cebu, inc.
M.L. Quezon St., Casuntingan, Mandaue 6014, Cebu
TEL: (6332) 346.4141 to 43
FAX: (6332) 346.3674
EMAIL: laline@craftersofcebu.com

daniele furniture, corp.
Sitio Libo, Tayud, Consolacion 6001, Cebu
TEL: (6332) 424.8391; 424.8392; 424.6526; 424.8752
FAX: (6332) 424.8752
EMAIL: averil@ danielefurniture.net
WEBSITE: www.danielefurniture.net

dedon manufacturing inc.
Zone 7, Birds of Paradise, Riverside, Canduman,
Mandaue 6014, Cebu
TEL: (6332) 328.9999 loc 170
FAX: (6332) 344.3600 local 01 & 02; 344.3602
EMAIL: info@dedon.ph;
janice.german@dedon.ph
WEBSITE: www.dedon.de

design ventures cebu, inc.
Upper Tingub, Mandaue 6014, Cebu
TEL: (6332) 346.0819; 346.0821
FAX: (6332) 346.0821
EMAIL: apalao@designventures.com.ph
WEBSITE: www.designventures.com.ph

detalia aurora inc.
Zone Paliya, Pakna-an, Mandaue 6014, Cebu
TEL: (6332) 420.4556; 420.6591; 420.6593
FAX: (6332) 420.4824
EMAIL: marketing@detaliaaurora.com
WEBSITE: www.detaliaaurora.com

diamond cane international, inc.
H. Abellana St., Canduman, Mandaue 6014, Cebu
TEL: (6332) 346.6332; 236.3404
FAX: (6332) 343.6383
EMAIL: diamondcane@pldtdsl.net;
info@diamondcanefurniture.com

elisons artcraft (export) industries, inc.
Barangay Tingub, Mandaue 6014, Cebu
TEL: (6332) 343.9726; 236.3432
FAX: (6332) 343.9724
EMAIL: elisons@pldtdsl.net

enpekei international, inc.
H. Abellana Ext., Pagsabungan, Mandaue 6014, Cebu
TEL: (6332) 236.0415; 512.3588
FAX: (6332) 236.0415
EMAIL: enpekei@pldtdsl.net;
enpekei@yahoo.com

equinox designs corp.
Corner Tupas and JM Basa St., Cebu Business Park,
Mandaue 6014, Cebu

TEL: (6332) 261.7282
FAX: (6332) 262.8150
EMAIL: edwinlu.equinox@gmail.com

eurowood products & technique mfg. corp.
Barangay Guinsay, Danao 6014, Cebu
TEL: (6332) 344.0160; 346.0407; 200.3881; 200.4381
FAX: (6332) 346.0407; 200.3881
EMAIL: eurowood@furniture-asia-export.com;
pcfr@mozcom.com
WEBSITE: www.furniture-asia-export.com

f&r ceniza family trading corp.
Upper Tingub, Mandaue 6014, Cebu
TEL: (6332) 343.7030; 343.9678
FAX: (6332) 343.6903
EMAIL: jmc@fossilstonefurniture.com;
jerceni_13@yahoo.com
WEBSITE: www.fossilstonefurniture.com

ferns finewood furniture inc.
Basak, Ibabao, Lapu-Lapu 6015, Cebu
TEL: (6332) 495.6193; 238.3116
FAX: (6332) 495.6193
EMAIL: ferns123ph@yahoo.com

finali furniture & home accessories, inc.
Riverside, Canduman, Mandaue 6014, Cebu
TEL: (6332) 236.4706
FAX: (6332) 346.4706
EMAIL: info@finalifurniture.ph;
rbsalazar2004@yahoo.com
WEBSITE: www.finalifurniture.ph

gecar metal solutions, inc.
Mindanao Rattan Compound, P. Burgos St. Alang-alang
Mandaue 6014, Cebu

TEL: (6332) 505.3505
FAX: (6332) 420.8828
EMAIL: gecar_gms@yahoo.com;
g_lao2004@yahoo.com

giardini del sole manufacturing & trading corp.
MQ Cuizon St., Alang-alang, Mandaue 6014, Cebu
TEL: (6332) 420.3933; 345.9579; 420.3242;
420.3465; 420.3960
FAX: (6332) 345.4370; 420.3933; 420.3960
EMAIL: giardini@pldtdsl.net;
giardinifurniture.accounting@gmail.com

global outdoor furniture supplies, inc.
777-B. Cuizon Compound, Upper San Vincente, Lilo-an
Mandaue 6014, Cebu
TEL: (6332) 401.8767
FAX: (6332) 401.8767
EMAIL: globaloutdoorfurniture@gmail.com;
cebucontractfurniture@gmail.com
WEBSITE: www.globaloutdoorfurniture.com

hacienda crafts company, Inc.
ANP Showroom, Lacson St., Bacolod 6100,
Negros Occidental
TEL: (6334) 213.0062
FAX: (6334) 432.3853; 434.1000
EMAIL: info@haciendacrafts.com
WEBSITE: www.haciendacrafts.com

heritage muebles mirabile export, inc.
Soong I, Mactan, Lapu-Lapu 6015, Cebu
TEL: (6332) 341.3822; 495.8016 to 18
FAX: (6332) 495.8015
EMAIL: heritage_67@yahoo.com
WEBSITE: www.heritagefurniture.com

highlight metal craft, inc.
Fuente Road, Guisi, Agus,
Lapu-Lapu 6015, Cebu
TEL: (6332) 495.3987
FAX: (6332) 495.3987
EMAIL: hlmc@globelines.com.ph

horizon international manufacturing inc.
East Binabag, Tayud, Consolacion 6001, Cebu
TEL: (6332) 423.3234; 424.4411
FAX: (6332) 423.3235
EMAIL: lmdelatorre@himi-furniture.com
WEBSITE: www.himi-furniture.com

insular rattan & native products, corp.
#31 J. P. Rizal St., Basak, Mandaue 6014, Cebu
TEL: (6332) 346.8822 to 24
FAX: (6332) 346.0653
EMAIL: insular@insularrattan.com
WEBSITE: www.insularrattan.com

interior basics export corporation
Lapu-Lapu 6015, Cebu
TEL: (6332) 341.3200; 341.3205; 516.7711
FAX: (6332) 341.3203
EMAIL: hr@interiorbasics.com.ph;
admin@interiorbasics.com.ph
WEBSITE: www.interiorbasics.com

interior crafts of the islands inc.
3-A General Maxilom Ave.
Cebu 6000, Cebu
TEL: (6332) 233.3056; 233.4045
FAX: (6332) 231.2555
EMAIL: info@kennethcobonpue.com;
paolo@kennethcobonpue.com
WEBSITE: www.kennethcobonpue.com

interphil marketing
H. Abellana St. Basak, Canduman,
Mandaue 6014, Cebu
TEL: (6332) 343.6696; 236.0165
FAX: (6332) 422.1791
EMAIL: interphil@pldtdsl.net

jamaica markets corporation
Castilex Compound, M.L. Quezon St.,
Cabancalan, Mandaue 6014, Cebu
TEL: (6332) 344.8166; 344.9128
FAX: (6332) 344.9128
EMAIL: jamaica@pacific.net.ph;
acctg@jamaicamarket.com

janice minor export inc.
Brgy. Calawisan, Lapu-Lapu 6015, Cebu
TEL: (6332) 340.0886; 341.5398
FAX: (6332) 340.0887
EMAIL: info@janiceminor.com
WEBSITE: www.janiceminor.com

jlq international, inc.
Upper Tingub, Tabok, Mandaue 6014, Cebu
TEL: (6332) 344.0229; 345.3940
FAX: (6332) 345.3940
EMAIL: nmongcopa@jlqintl.com;
lita_jlq@hotmail.com
WEBSITE: www.jlqintl.com

josephine fine arts industries
Tawason St., Canduman, Mandaue 6014, Cebu
TEL: (6332) 422.1216; 422.1215; 406.7658
FAX: (6332) 422.1215
EMAIL: jfinearts@skyinet.net;
jfinearts@gmail.com

kirsten international phils., inc.
Tayud, Lilo-an 6002, Cebu
TEL: (6332) 232.1179; 231.9130
FAX: (6332) 231.9130
EMAIL: ceo@kirsten-intl.com
WEBSITE: www.kirsten-intl.com

lenbert manufacturing, inc.
H. Abellana St., Jagobiao, Mandaue 6014, Cebu
TEL: (6332) 345.8034 to 36
FAX: (6332) 345.8037
EMAIL: rainorshine@lenbertfurniture.com
WEBSITE: www.lenbertfurniture.com

lionel lights & lamp
64 Sen. Gil Puyat Ave., Makati 1200, Manila
TEL: (632) 844.1236
FAX: (632) 845.0177
EMAIL: lionellights@yahoo.com;
sales@lionellightsandlamps.com
WEBSITE: www.lionellightsandlamps.com

mactan wood carving and
gilding corporation
Creative Building #2 MEPZ 1 Gate 5, Lapu-Lapu 6015, Cebu
TEL: (6332) 239.2381
FAX: (6332) 239.2381
EMAIL: info@mwcgco.com
WEBSITE: www.mwcgco.com

maitland-smith cebu
Mactan Economic Zone 1, Gate 2, Lapu-Lapu 6015, Cebu
TEL: (6332) 340.0277
FAX: (6332) 340.0266
EMAIL: pabernathy@maitland-smith.com.ph;
ibasco@maitland-smith-rohq.com.ph

mastercraft phils., inc.
438 Burgos St., Alang-alang, Mandaue 6014, Cebu
TEL: (6332) 346.7217; 238.8111; 238.8555;
236.0853; 236.0128
FAX: (6332) 236.0071, 346.7217, 238.8222
EMAIL: marketing@mendco.com.ph;
marketing@mastercraftph.com
WEBSITE: www.mendco.com.ph

mehitabel furniture inc.
Tac-an Road, Talamban, Cebu 6000
TEL: (6332) 2314039; 4167000; 4160152; 414.7000
FAX: (6332) 2313478; 3441063; 4167006
EMAIL: rbooth@mehitabel.com.ph;
jbooth@mehitabel.com.ph

mobilia products, inc.
MEPZ 1, Gate 1, Lapu-Lapu 6015, Cebu
TEL: (6332) 340.0496; 340.3346
FAX: (6332) 340.0497
EMAIL: boowy@mobilia.ph
WEBSITE: www.mobilia.com

murillo's export international, inc.
Lower Inayawan, Cebu 6000, Cebu
TEL: (6332) 273.0681; 273.7077; 318.5625
FAX: (6332) 272.0296; 273.0681
EMAIL: allan@murillo.ph
WEBSITE: www.murillo.ph

nature's legacy eximport, inc.
Upper Cogon, Compostella 6003, Cebu
TEL: (6332) 425.8399; 425.8814
FAX: (6332) 425.8815
EMAIL: info@natureslegacy.com
WEBSITE: www.natureslegacy.com

ncb industries
Greenhills Road, Cabancalan,
Mandaue 6014, Cebu
TEL: (6332) 345.4294
FAX: (6332) 345.4294
EMAIL: pilipinazcrafts_ncbindustries@yahoo.com

nicey export corporation
#168 Upper Tingub, Mandaue 6014, Cebu
TEL: (6332) 346.6855; 479.9603
FAX: (6332) 346.6855
EMAIL: jtenario@yahoo.com
WEBSITE: www.niceyexport.com

obra cebuana inc.
Arcenas Compound, R. Duterte St.,
Banawa, Cebu 6000
TEL: (6332) 261.2939; 261.2844
FAX: (6332) 253.1621
EMAIL: obracebuana@gmail.com
WEBSITE: www.obracebuana.com

okiberry ventures corporation
Fuentes Road, Guisi, Agus,
Lapu-Lapu 6015, Cebu
TEL: (6332) 340.7492; 495.3207
FAX: (6332) 495.3093
EMAIL: sales@okiberry.com
WEBSITE: www.okiberry.com

pacific traders & manufacturing corp.
P.C. Suico St., Tabok, Mandaue 6014, Cebu
TEL: (6332) 346.0083; 346.8263; 344.3607
FAX: (6332) 346.0952; 346.3315
EMAIL: csg@pacific-traders.com
WEBSITE: www.pacific-traders.com

paragon export
Carajay, Gun-ob, Lapu-Lapu 6015, Cebu
TEL: (6332) 341.0434
FAX: (6332) 341.0435
EMAIL: michael@dekorattex.com;
yoeri.dochez@dekorattex.be
WEBSITE: www.dekorattex.com

peba trading & mfg. corporation
Kagudoy Rd., Basak, Lapu-Lapu 6015, Cebu
TEL: (6332) 340.5738 to 39
FAX: (6332) 340.5739
EMAIL: peba@mozcom.com

san gabriel metal concepts, inc.
Door 8, LK Bldg., Tipolo, Mandaue 6014, Cebu
TEL: (6332) 422.5942; 422.5943; 345.2817
FAX: (6332) 422.5947
EMAIL: info@sgmci.com; sales@sgmci.com;
admin@sgmci.com
WEBSITE: www.sgmci.com

sason shop inc.
Brgy. Alijis, P.O. Box 922, Bacolod 6100,
Negros Occidental
TEL: (6334) 435.4759
FAX: (6334) 708.7979
EMAIL: info@sasonshop.com
WEBSITE: www.sasonshop.com

scarborough fine furniture inc.
Lot 2, Blk 9, MEPZ 2, Basak, Lapu-Lapu 6015, Cebu
TEL: (6332) 341.5152 to 54
FAX: (6332) 341.5134
EMAIL: sffi@scarffi.com.ph; aida@scarffi.com.ph
WEBSITE: www.scarffi.com.ph

simon crafts international, inc.
#10 S. E. Jayme St., Pakna-an,
Mandaue 6014, Cebu
TEL: (6332) 420.6500; 346.1589; 346.1589
FAX: (6332) 346.1589
EMAIL: simoncrafts@simoncrafts.com

sky shine furniture designs
Bagong Daan, Yati, Tayud, Lilo-an 6002, Cebu
TEL: (6332) 424.6076; 495.9235
EMAIL: info@skyshinefd.com;
soo856@skyshinefd.com
WEBSITE: www.skyshinefd.com

stonesets international inc.
Don Sergio Suico St., Canduman,
Mandaue 6014, Cebu
TEL: (6332) 422.1601; 422.1633; 422.1675
FAX: (6332) 344.7600
EMAIL: info@vitoselma.com;
eds626@yahoo.com
WEBSITE: www.vitoselma.com

stoneworld impex, inc.
Tingub St., Mandaue 6014, Cebu
TEL: (6332) 346.3762
FAX: (6332) 346.4491
EMAIL: janet_stoneworld@yahoo.com;
janet_tvs@yahoo.com
WEBSITE: www.stoneworldimpex.com

superior ex/import product, inc.
E-005 Cansojong, Talisay 6045, Cebu
TEL: (6332) 491.8807; 236.5964
FAX: (6332) 273.0774
EMAIL: superior@globelines.com.ph

tala cebu furniture
manufacturing inc.
P. Basubas St. Tipolo, Mandaue 6014, Cebu
TEL: (6332) 236.5828
FAX: (6332) 236.5828
EMAIL: lin.talahome@gmail.com
WEBSITE: www.talacontract.com

tequesta international inc.
Ibabao, Agus, Lapu-Lapu 6015, Cebu
TEL: (6332) 238.5700 to 02
FAX: (6332) 238.5703
EMAIL: tequesta@smartbro.net

the classical touch ventures, inc.
Hi-way Pakna-an, Mandaue 6014, Cebu
TEL: (6332) 422.6204; 344.5958; 420.4154
FAX: (6332) 422.6204
EMAIL: alan@theclassicaltouch.com;
classical_touch@yahoo.com
WEBSITE: www.theclassicaltouch.com

tradewinds rattan & handicraft, inc.
P. Remedio St., Banilad, Mandaue 6014, Cebu
TEL: (6332) 3447954
FAX: (6332) 344.7954
EMAIL: tri_mktg@pldtdsl.net;
debbie@tradewinds.com.ph
WEBSITE: www.tradewinds.com.ph

tumandok crafts industries
Purok Maria Morena, Brgy. Calumangan,
Bago, Negros Occidental
TEL: (6334) 434.2632; 707.7174;
731.0026; 476.1059
FAX: (6334) 434.2632; 707.7174; 731.0026

EMAIL: tumadok_crafts@yahoo.com;
tumandok.crafts@gmail.com
WEBSITE: www.tumandok.com

venus crafts corporation
168 Hyram Bldg., Cotcot, Lilo-an 6002, Cebu
TEL: (6332) 424.8113
FAX: (6332) 424.8113
EMAIL: info@venuscrafts.com
WEBSITE: www.venuscrafts.com

wicker & vine, inc.
PC Suico St., Tingub, Mandaue 6014, Cebu
TEL: (6332) 236.8603
FAX: (6332) 236.8746
EMAIL: mainbox@wickerandvine.com

wire works international, Inc.
923 Labogon Road, Basak, Mandaue 6014, Cebu
TEL: (6332) 420.6769
FAX: (6332) 420.6769
EMAIL: wireworks@globelines.com.ph;
wireworksph@gmail.com
WEBSITE: www.wireworksph.com

woven furniture designs inc.
Caimito St., Purok Narra, Simboryo Tayud,
Lilo-an 6002, Cebu
TEL: (6332) 406.8308; 406.8312; 564.3794
FAX: (6332) 564.3794
EMAIL: info@wovenfurnituredesigns.com
WEBSITE: www.wovenfurnituredesigns.com

acknowledgments

writer

Ms. Maricris Encarnacion is the publisher and executive editor of *Where At Cebu*, a Cebu lifestyle destination magazine. She is a regular contributor to Metro Society, a leading magazine of the media group ABS-CBN Inc.

Married to Raul Encarnacion and mother to Beau Encarnacion, Maricris, who is also a businesswoman, has taken to writing as her second career which she believes holds the key to her many voyages of discovery in life's great adventure.

editors

Ms. Karen Singson
Ms. Michelle White

photographers

Ms. Medal Elepaño
Mr. Ted Madamba
Ms. Patricia Mancao

cfif

Ms. Cheryl Judilla
Ms. Laurie Lobaton

alenter cane/ambiente designs intl. inc.

Mr. Bernard Alegrado
Mr. Eddie Alegrado

apy cane incorporated

Ms. Noreen Yu

arden classic inc.

Mr. Arden Siarot
Ms. Jen Siarot

atillo's rattan/florentino III

Ms. Irma Atillo

bon-ace fashion tools, inc.

Mr. Ramir Bonghanoy

castilex industrial corporation

Ms. Laurie Boquiren

cebu fil-veneer corporation

Mr. Carlo Cordaro

cebu intertrade export

Ms. Grace Guinefolleau

classical geometry export trading

Mr. Clayton Tugonon

coast pacific manufacturing corp.

Ms. Tina Lo

cosonsa mfg., inc.

Ms. Ellen Galan
Mr. Pride Sasser

dedon manufacturing inc.

Mr. Herve Lampert
Mr. Vince Lampert
Ms. Love Joy Malicay
Ms. Constanze von Mühlenfels

dekeyser and friends

Ms. Lotte Danacker
Mr. Florian Hoffman
Mr. Rouven Steinfeld

design ventures cebu, inc.

Ms. Kae Batiqui
Mr. Agustin Palao
Ms. Debbie Palao

interior crafts of the islands inc.

Ms. Betty Cobonpue
Mr. Kenneth Cobonpue
Mr. Paolo Konst

infini collection
Ms. Margueritte Lhuillier

janice minor export inc.
Ms. Janice Minor

jcl export inc.
Mr. Fernando Gohuisiong

maitland-smith cebu
Mr. Preston Abernathy
Ms. Ivy Marie Basco
Ms. Daniela Cases
Ms. Divah Galeon

mcguire furniture company
Ms. Catherine Wilkes

mehitabel furniture inc.
Mrs. Josephine A. Booth
Mr. Robert Louise Booth

mendco/mastercraft phils inc.
Mr. Phillip Lim
Mr. Eric Ng Mendoza

mindanao rattan corp/
reunion furnishings/detalia aurora inc.
Mr. Guillermo Rodriguez
Ms. Paula Rodriguez
Mr. Efren Sarmiento
Ms. Luisa de los Santos-Robinson

nature's legacy eximport, inc.
Ms. Edsel Buenavista
Mr. Pedro Delantar

obra cebuana inc.
Mr. Edwin Rivera
Mr. Rene Ybañez

outlook (philippines) international ltd.
Ms. Louwee Sarausad

pacific traders & manufacturing corp.
Ms. Lorelei Mingoy
Ms. Bernice Montenegro
Mr. Charles Streegan
Ms. Greece Suico
Mr. Fernando "Astik" Villarin

QF Gamallo
Mr. Apollo Gamallo
Ms. Irene Gamallo

ralph lauren
Ms. Jamie Bahar
Mr. Calvin Churchman
Ms. Sophie Goodwillie

raphael legacy inc.
Mr. Charles Belleza
Mr. Victor Guerra

rattan originals inc./
casa cebuana incorporada
Ms. Angela F. Paulin

stonesets international inc.
Mr. Bim Bacaltos
Ms. Vicky Keys
Mr. Jim LaBarge
Mr. Graham Maitland-Smith
Mr. Alan Palecek

Ms. Ruby Babao-Salutan
Ms. Evelyn Selma
Mr. Vito Selma
Mr. Richard Stolzman
Dan Wisterhuff, Jr.
Dan Wisterhuff, Sr.
Ms. Corito Yu

Home accessories by young Cebu designers were among the attractions at Cebu Next 2011. Left to right: Designs by Stanley Ruiz – Branch floor lamp for Hacienda Crafts Company, Inc.; Hexagon bottled jar, Trapezoid bottled jar, and Barrel end table for Crafters of Cebu, Inc.